France in an Age of Globalization

FRANCE
in an Age of
Globalization

Hubert Védrine *with Dominique Moïsi*

Translated by Philip H. Gordon

BROOKINGS INSTITUTION PRESS
Washington, D.C.

Originally published as *Les cartes de la France à l'heure de la mondialisation*
Copyright © 2000 Librairie Arthème Fayard

Copyright © 2001
THE BROOKINGS INSTITUTION
1775 *Massachusetts Avenue, N.W., Washington, D.C. 20036*
www.brookings.edu

Library of Congress Cataloging-in-Publication data

Védrine, Hubert.
    [Cartes de la France à l'heure de la mondialisation. English]
    France in an age of globalization / Hubert Védrine with Dominique Moïsi;
translated by Philip H. Gordon.
        p.   cm.
Includes index.
    ISBN 0-8157-0007-5 (alk. paper)
    1. France—Foreign relations—1981- 2. France—Foreign relations—
United States. 3. United States—Foreign relations—France.
4. United States—Foreign relations—1993- 5. Védrine, Hubert.
6. Moïsi, Dominique. 7. World politics—1995-2005. 8. Globalization.
I. Moïsi, Dominique. II. Title.
DC423 .V428 2001   2001001704
    327.4407

9 8 7 6 5 4 3 2 1

The paper used in this publication meets minimum requirements of the American National Standard for Information Sciences—Permanence of Paper for Printed Library Materials: ANSI Z39.48-1992.

Typeset in Adobe Caslon

Composition and design by Lawrence Converse

Printed by R. R. Donnelley and Sons
Harrisonburg, Virginia

Contents

Preface

"AT DEMOCRACY'S PICNIC, PARIS SUPPLIES ANTS," read the June 27, 2000, headline in the *New York Times*. The story referred to the previous day's meeting of 107 countries in Warsaw, Poland, to declare the creation of a Community of Democracies, a sort of pressure group for the promotion of democracy around the world. The summit, featuring the participation of then U.S. secretary of state Madeleine Albright and a number of foreign ministers, was the culmination of a process, led by the United States, that had been going on for nearly a year. At the end of the meeting, 106 of the countries present signed a declaration instituting the new community. The one participant who refused to sign on behalf of his country was the French foreign minister, Hubert Védrine.

For many in Washington at the time—not least at the State Department, which had conceived of the Community of Democracies and which has always had a sort of love-hate relationship with the French—the rebuff was "typical."

Since democracy was obviously a good thing, the only possible grounds for Védrine's action must have been to take an opportunity to poke a stick in the eye of the United States, denying its role as natural leader of the post–cold war world. Védrine, after all, had not only been an active proponent of a more "multipolar" world, but had even coined a new word—*hyperpuissance* ("hyperpower")—to describe the post–cold war United States.

Védrine's own take on the Warsaw episode—his skepticism about "instant democracy," his belief that Western countries should get their own houses in order before preaching to others, his aversion to seeing France drafted into a new crusade for democracy, however noble the cause—is just one of the many fascinating passages to be found in the discussion that follows. That discussion is the product of numerous hours that Védrine spent, in repeated sittings, with Dominique Moïsi, a noted author and deputy director at the French Institute for International Relations, also well known for his regular columns for the *Financial Times*. Moïsi was given free range to press Védrine on any subject he liked, and even—as is clear in the later chapters—to challenge the foreign minister to defend his "realism," which Moïsi, a strong advocate of both international morality and European integration, seems to think is excessive.

An earlier, French-language version of this work was published under the title *Les Cartes de la France à l'heure de la mondialisation* (France's assets in an age of globalization) in spring 2000. The present English-language version adds extensive new material and covers many important developments since the French version came out, including Védrine's assessments of the 2000 U.S. presidential election; the July–December 2000 French presidency of the EU (including the outcome of the Nice Summit); the breakdown of the Middle East peace process; developments in Russia, Africa, and Asia; and much more. That Védrine was extremely diligent in keeping the book up to date I know all too well; as director of the Brookings Center on the United States and France and the translator of this project, I had to scramble along with the authors to deal with significant new material as important events occurred through the spring of 2001.

There are too many important themes in this wide-ranging book to comment on here, but let me just note three that stand out. The first is the degree to which the United States, in both positive and negative ways, permeates Védrine and Moïsi's discussion. This is true not just in the chapter on "How to Deal with the United States?" but throughout the book, beginning (not by chance) with the references in the very first pages to the ideas of two American authors, Francis Fukuyama and Samuel Huntington. The ubiquity of the United States in this discussions is no doubt a function of American hyperpower—the fact that the United States is, as Védrine says, "predominant in all areas: economic, technological, military, monetary, linguistic, [and] cultural." But it is also, I believe, a function of France's own history. As a former great power itself, whose language, military strength, economic influence and culture once had a presence all around the globe, France probably feels American dominance more than any of its neighbors in Europe. (Would it occur to many other European foreign ministers, for example, to rank the countries of the world, as Védrine does in the opening chapter?) It is thus not surprising that, even though this discussion was originally intended for publication only in France, the relationship with the United States is one of its dominant themes.

The second theme that stands out is globalization, which Védrine candidly recognizes to be a particular challenge for France. To be sure, the original title of the book referred to France's "assets" in the age of globalization, which Védrine believes to be many: it is one of the world's most productive economies, it is a significant military power, it has an attractive culture (which pulled in 75 million tourists last year, the most in the world), it has special relations with parts of Africa and the Middle East, and it plays an influential role in the European Union, to name just a few. But he also admits that many aspects of globalization—neo-liberal economics, the English language, the need for individualism and flexibility, and certain legal and accounting practices—actually suit the Americans (them again) much more than the French. Among the most interesting and potentially important contributions of this book are Védrine's ideas on how to manage globalization—through the strengthening of institutions and the creation of rules to govern trade, finance, and geopolitics—so that its benefits can be more evenly distributed and to avoid a public backlash. Some Americans, determined to keep government and international institutions out of economic and political life, will view these ideas with suspicion, but they cannot be ignored. As globalization continues to spread not only great wealth but also inequalities and insecurities around the world, Védrine's thinking on how to manage it could well find increasing support, including in the United States.

Finally, in reading these pages one cannot help but be struck by what might be called Védrine's "certain idea of France," to borrow the expression used in the first sentence of General Charles de Gaulle's war memoirs. This is obviously not to say that there is no difference between the views of the French foreign minister at the dawn of the twenty-first century and those of the great World War II hero who was France's president from 1959–69. However, even as Védrine perceptively analyzes and insists on the need to adapt to new phenomena like globalization and European integration, his thoughts also demonstrate the remarkable continuity in French foreign policy thinking over fifty years: the preoccupation with the United States; the desire to play a global diplomatic role; the determination to preserve a distinctive French culture; the willingness to be different, even when this means clashing with the Americans; and the desire to fight for the peoples and countries in the world whom no one else will fight for. Thus even as he exhorts his compatriots to get over their obsession with France's glorious past, Védrine himself is not in the least prepared to abdicate what he sees as France's ability and duty to continue to play a major geopolitical role. "As far as the eye can see," he tells Moïsi, "I am convinced there will be a global French foreign policy." No one reading this book, or who follows French affairs on regular basis, for that matter, will be inclined to disagree.

In the pages that follow there are countless other interesting and important issues—Védrine's vision of Europe, the debate about military intervention, the role of ethics in foreign policy, French policy in the Middle East, and many more—that readers will form their own opinions on. Americans will not agree with everything that Hubert Védrine has to say about these matters, but they will surely appreciate his remarkable efforts to explain his thinking and to engage openly and honestly with the American public on some of the most important issues of our time. France is a crucial partner of the United States. And as difficult as it can be—for reasons that Védrine helps to explain here—it is also one of a very few countries in the world that not only shares basic American values but has the resources and willingness to stand with the United States to defend them. On the range of issues raised in this book, there is much more that brings the Americans and French together than there is that divides them.

Hubert Védrine would like to thank his press and communications adviser, Caroline Malaussena, and the rest of his staff for their assistance with this project. The authors and I are also grateful for the valuable contributions made by Bridget Alway, Tanjam Jacobson, Aurélie Johnson, Mary Mortensen, Carlotta Ribar, Gunnar Trumbull, and Justin Vaïsse.

PHILIP H. GORDON

France in an Age of Globalization

The World Today

DOMINIQUE MOÏSI: More than ten years after the fall of the Berlin Wall, how would you characterize the world we live in? How does it differ from the cold war world?

HUBERT VÉDRINE: Let's begin with the most obvious: the symbolic end of the world that emerged from World War II occurred with the fall of the Berlin Wall in November 1989. The real end of that world came with Mikhail Gorbachev's resignation and the dissolution of the Soviet Union in December 1991. The years 1989–91 marked the end of the bipolar Soviet-American world, of the cold war, and of détente. The global world we live in now requires new analysis.

MOÏSI: Is it the "end of history," as Francis Fukuyama said at the end of the cold war?

VÉDRINE: I understand why one might want to draw attention to these radical changes, but I never bought into that thesis. History was "unfrozen" by the end of the cold war. There are nearly forty conflicts today, including twenty in Africa, and economic competition has gotten worse. I don't think that the progressive extension of democracy and market economies is enough to end conflict. Samuel Huntington's thesis about the risks of conflict in the areas where civilizations meet is not so far off the mark, even if it is a bit too schematic. Look at the line that goes from Kosovo to Sinkiang and Jolo.

Moïsi: Is the current world unipolar or multipolar?

Védrine: With the breakup of the Soviet Union, it's decompartmentalized. I'd say it's nearly global. The market economy has no competition. No countermodels exist any more. China isn't one. In this nearly unified world, one can't deny that there is henceforth a dominant "pole," the United States. In this sense the world is unipolar—even if it's potentially multipolar.

Among the 189 countries in the world today, one constitutes a category all by itself, notwithstanding the formal equality of states of the United Nations. I'm talking about the United States, the world's only "hyperpower." The United States is predominant in all areas: economic, technological, military, monetary, linguistic, cultural. This situation is unprecedented: what previous empire subjugated the entire world, including its adversaries? Moreover, while U.S. domination may be the result of a project—for example when the United States assailed its allies' colonial empires—it is certainly not the result of a plot. The Americans were called to the Old Continent by the Europeans in 1917, then again in 1944. After 1945, at the request of the Europeans, they stayed there, despite their periodic bouts of isolationism. Their domination was fueled by others' fiascoes, which seemed to justify the providential role—so-called manifest destiny—they had ascribed to themselves. And here they are now, having become a hyperpower. (The word "superpower" seems to me too closely linked to the cold war and military issues.)

When I started using this term, in 1998, some Americans thought it aggressive, since in English the prefix *hyper-* has a negative connotation, as in "hyperactive." Some even claimed to see in the use of this term the resurgence of a systematically critical attitude toward the United States, supposedly typical of France. This is clearly not the case.

In French, *hyper-* is a neutral term. It simply means very big or very much, even more than the prefix *super-*. My objective was thus not to be negative toward the United States, but to get French people to think about the current state of the world. I think Americans who are interested in France now understand this. Besides, I have since learned that an American writer, Ben Wattenberg, had already in 1990 used the term in the same sense. He now prefers the term "omnipower," but it's the same idea.

Moïsi: Is globalization the same thing as Americanization? Why does the United States seem to be like a fish in water in this new global world?

Védrine: "Like a fish in water" is exactly the right expression. The United States is a very big fish that swims easily and rules supreme in the waters of globalization. Again, globalization is not the completion of an American plan, even if it is the case that the big American firms have supported it and are profiting greatly from it. The United States, it is true, is pursuing an Open Door commercial policy, which was Britain's policy in the nineteenth century. (It was, of course, someone else's door that was open!) Americans get great benefits from this for a large number of reasons: because of their economic size; because globalization takes place in their language; because it is organized along neoliberal economic principles; because they impose their legal, accounting, and technical practices; and because they're advocates of individualism. They also benefit because they posses what the writer and philosopher René Girard has called the "mental power" to inspire the dreams and desires of others, thanks to their mastery of global images through film and television and because, for these same reasons, large numbers of students from other countries come to the United States to finish their studies.

Moïsi: Doesn't America's real power lie as much in the dynamism of U.S. society as in traditional measures of power? Indeed, couldn't you even say that America is powerful despite—rather than because of—Washington and American policy? Isn't America's "soft power"—the power to convince others and the power to attract people to the American model—in this sense greater than its "hard power"—the power to compel others to act? You sometimes see this in times of international crisis.

VÉDRINE: But these two types of power reinforce each other! This is what I mean when I talk about the Pentagon, the English language, Hollywood, CNN, the Internet, American culture, etc. Soft power, in any case, is not entirely new. The way Santa Claus is now represented throughout the world is thanks to an advertisement for Coca-Cola in the 1930s. Today it's the diffusion of Halloween that is striking. This magnetism results from a combination of economic and human vitality—seventeen years of growth!—of technological and cultural creativity, of an abundance of resources and the size of the internal market, of myths and reality. American policy expresses and projects this influence, reinforced by the conviction of fulfilling a providential mission on behalf of humanity. But the American political system is becoming less and less capable of shielding elections, and thus democracy, from the law of money and lobbies. (Is not the ultimate logic of the market economy that *everything* is for sale?) Torn between isolationism and hegemony, weakened by abstention, often hindered by tensions between the White House and Congress, this system is a serious handicap for the United States itself, and therefore a problem for everyone. Not to mention the role of Supreme Court judges.

MOÏSI: Alongside the special case of the United States, what category do countries like France and Great Britain—the former great powers—belong to? How can they be defined? Is there a sort of first class for the United States, and then second, third, and even fourth classes for the others? Have the French become second-class passengers on history's new train?

VÉDRINE: I don't see things that way. Following the United States, there are some 188 other countries. At the top of this list are seven of what I would call "globally influential powers," a diverse group of large countries that have certain attributes of power and a range of means to influence the world. In this category I would put France, Britain, Germany, Russia, China, Japan, as well as India (especially as it broadens its still regional vision). That is why, when I speak to the French public, I try to persuade it to be neither pretentious nor uselessly nostalgic, but also not to devalue itself or underestimate what

France is today. I try to contribute to a serene and balanced perception of reality.

The case of Europe—power or region?—remains to be determined. Other countries have the potential to join this group. The relevant criteria include gross national product (GNP); the level of technology; nuclear weapons, even if some would want to downgrade this factor; membership of the UN Security Council, the G-8, the European Union; the role of a country's language; cultural influence; influence derived from history; and future potential. There is thus no reason for the French to be gloomy!

MOÏSI: You could classify or qualify things differently.

VÉDRINE: Sure, you could focus exclusively on geographical size, population, nuclear status, permanent membership of the UN Security Council; or on GNP—using these criteria France would be fourth, behind the United States, Japan, and Germany. Personally, however, I try to include and synthesize all aspects of power—whether they be modern or ancient, tangible or intangible, hard or soft.

MOÏSI: Should the countries that you just listed all one day become permanent members of the UN Security Council?

VÉDRINE: Germany, Japan, and India, among others, belong on a reformed Security Council as new permanent or nonpermanent members, so that it really represents today's world, not just the northern hemisphere. Thus also including Latin America, Africa, and the Arab world. It will also be necessary to maintain its effectiveness by preserving the use of the veto but also making more responsible use of it, since the world needs a credible and effective Security Council more than ever before.

MOÏSI: How would you classify other powers?

VÉDRINE: After the globally influential powers, you've got a certain number of "powers" in the true sense of the word. Without question, Australia, Indonesia, Brazil, Mexico, South Africa, Nigeria, Egypt, Iran, Turkey, Israel, Italy, Spain, Poland, to cite only these examples, belong to this group. I would say there are about twenty to thirty such countries. I would also put in this group other countries that get their means to act from their membership in the G-8—Canada, for example—or the European Union.

Moïsi: And after this group?

Védrine: After these powers, you come to a set of countries that have neither the power nor the means to influence the situation around them. Normal countries, if you will, but which are often dependent on others.

Finally, you could add a category of "pseudostates," which have emerged from a type of proliferation that nobody talks about very much, the proliferation of sovereignty: there were eight states at the Congress of Vienna in 1815, there were fifty-five in 1946, and there are 189 today. (The French analyst Pascal Boniface has done some interesting work on this.) These are states that are incapable of effectively exercising their formal sovereignty and live off international aid—"failed states," if you will. They too often fall prey to the sorts of transnational forces—legal or illegal—that globalization has intensified. "Microstates," of which there are a few dozen, are also a problem, though there are some microstates that are stable and prosperous.

Moïsi: Is this system, where you've got four categories of state actors—one hyperpower, a few globally influential powers, some countries that simply exist, and some pseudostates (not to mention nonstate actors)—more or less stable than previous systems?

Védrine: The word "system" implies that all of this has been thought through. We're a long way from that. This world is marked by an unquestionable extension of democracy, which is great. But it is potentially unstable for several reasons: because it no longer has the iron discipline that prevailed when there were two antagonistic camps that mutually deterred each other; because of the proliferation of states that I spoke about earlier; as a consequence of the ambivalent development of nonstate actors; and because the explosion of unequal wealth creates great international tensions.

Moïsi: Beyond the competition for excellence, is not one of the unique things about today's world the beginning of a transnational—and not just an international—group? Not only are there states belonging to very different categories, but there are other actors, like multinational companies and international organizations—not to speak of the beginnings of a civil society without borders—who now play a major role in the global balance. That's the new reality.

VÉDRINE: You're right: these are the new realities prevailing everywhere. They raise new questions that some contemporary Montesquieu, starting from scratch, could try to respond to. But the classical geopolitical questions have not therefore disappeared: Can American predominance last? Can Europe, destined to enlarge, become a world power, and if so, how? Will India one day be able to think and act on a global level? Will Russia become a great modern country, and if so, when? Can China transform itself without tragedy? Will other parts of the world, like Mercosur (the common market among Brazil, Argentina, Uruguay, Paraguay, and soon Chile), become poles?

But there, too, you've got a point: one cannot limit oneself to thinking about these "classical" questions, since new actors have emerged in the world as a consequence of the declining relative power of states. For better or for worse, these forces are changing international relations. This, too, is globalization.

Moïsi: Where does this globalization come from?

VÉDRINE: It comes from way back, having been driven by the spirit of conquest and technical progress. It advanced gradually for a long time before starting to advance exponentially, as is now the case. Short of going back to the Crusades, it was the European colonial expansion starting in the sixteenth century that marked the beginning of the globalization that we now see triumphant. More recently, there were the world wars (in fact the extension to the rest of the world of European conflicts), which led the United States to fulfill the role that it plays to this day.

Moïsi: At the end of the nineteenth century, with the revolution in transportation, there was already an early form of globalization, which people now tend to forget. In 1910 the economist Norman Angell (in his book *The Grand Illusion*) was persuaded that economic independence would make war impossible. This was less than four years before the Sarajevo assassination.

VÉDRINE: Indeed. Technical progress in the areas of transportation—from the compass to the rocket—and communications—from the telegraph to the Internet—is now fusing together. These have always been the motors of globalization, maybe the true motors. The world has been decompartmentalized ever since airplanes were invented. Information is now available at the same time all around the world by means that are nearly impossible to control. Distance has been abolished. Today's globalization is the product of technical progress and of the series of tragedies of the twentieth century.

MOÏSI: For you, does globalization mean the interdependence or the relative decline of states?

VÉDRINE: It means both. Contemporary societies are interdependent, some more dependent than others. They have been directed by governments that are themselves interdependent, whose role has been reduced—or at least redefined—and which are forced to act together to avoid being on the defensive. States have gone from being independent to being interdependent; they have to coordinate their actions. That has become so constraining that I sometimes compare this joint sovereignty to a tedious and interminable meeting of a tenants' association! But it's also a school in global democracy.

Another phenomenon—the growing interaction, to the point of being an obsession, between power and opinion—plays a part in this interdependence. The spread of information in real time provokes strong reactions, particularly in our fragmented and media-driven societies, where an increasingly isolated individual consumer is constantly bombarded by images and sounds, with clear emotional effects. This influences government.

MOÏSI: Do you think a true "international civil society," linked to the existence of globalization, is really emerging?

VÉDRINE: Yes. It's a nice idea, but international civil society is really a little bit of a jumble, or a mirage. There are more than humanitarian issues—usually quite admirable—involved. It's a mixed bag. You find a bit of everything—generosity, devotion, networks, militancy, interests, lobbies, beliefs, and a fair amount of disguised real power. Those who see a panacea in this phenomenon forget that it in no way gets rid of the hierarchies of power; it merely expresses them differently. The influential "civil societies" are necessarily those of the most powerful countries. Thus it's the civil societies and the NGOs (nongovernmental organizations) from the rich, media-driven countries that exercise the most influence in the world. They're the ones with the means to communicate, and thus the power to impose their views. It's American influence, not that of Niger, Bolivia, or Bangladesh. It's not Nigerian NGOs that are going to intervene in Northern Ireland or demonstrate in Seattle. The emergence of an international civil society modifies the way we wield power and political responsibility, for example, by making people pay attention to things like human rights, antipersonnel mines, and the environment. But it does not really modify the global balance of power, indeed far from it. Besides, many NGOs from the "south" are just extensions of NGO's from the "north."

MOÏSI: On the other hand, it reinforces the positive character of democracy as a system of expression and monitoring. Isn't globalization at least potentially a plus for democracy?

VÉDRINE: Yes, potentially, at least. In any case we have to move toward this goal. But globalization is not automatically good for democracy, because it was not democratically adopted. No one asks for it, even if it imposes itself on everyone. What is clear is that globalization is superficially accompanied by political democracy. But is it really fair to equate the emergence of an international civil society with the advancement of democracy? I don't think so, not if we let things go without making progress toward better regulation. Civil society is not made up of elected representatives but of active minorities and self-designated forces, which does not correspond to our democratic principles. This does not mean that certain groups do not do useful, sometimes admirable, work, but that in itself has no relationship to democracy. Look at the specific, even picky, demands that we make of countries where we want to help democracy stick: we verify the electoral lists, the conditions for running for office, the respect for equal speaking time, finances, the role of the media, etc. Are we supposed to ignore all this so long as there is some "civil society" in which someone has set up a website or created an association? What do we know about these 26,000 existing NGOs? What do we know about their work forces, their leaders, their resources, their recruiting, their working methods? A bit more transparency would be welcome! Let's take these forces and what they are expressing into account, but let's avoid confusing roles and responsibilities!

MOÏSI: But to sum up, is it progress or is it a risk? Jean-Marie Guéhenno has written about the "end of democracy" or the "democratic illusion."[1]

VÉDRINE: It's both progress and a risk. A lot of people think in zero-sum terms: development of civil society = the weakening of states = progress. Some activists, especially in the West, seem to be convinced that the weakening of states, allegedly oppressive by nature, is a good in and of itself. They seem to think that as soon as states get out of the way, the most beautiful democracy will emerge in this newly liberated space.... That's not exactly what has happened these last few years; in some ways it's often the jungle, not democracy, that has gained ground. Look at the coincidence between the end of the Soviet Union, financial globalization, and the explosion of organized crime! This new reality has to be analyzed without nostalgia, but also without naiveté.

Democracy is not like instant coffee, where you can just add water and stir. It doesn't result from a conversion, but from a process. The development of civil society is a fact. We should make it more responsible and support its most useful aspects, but for states to abdicate their roles would mean progress neither for democracy nor for what we in French call the "management of globalization."

MOÏSI: Is this why you refused, in France's name, to sign the Warsaw Declaration creating the Conference of Democracies? Many, especially in the United States, did not understand why you did this.

VÉDRINE: Madeleine Albright and Polish foreign minister Bronislav Geremek held a conference on democracy in Warsaw in June 2000. We're all in favor of democracy, but I was not too keen to go to this conference. As I said, democratization has always resulted from a process and not from a sudden conversion—internal maturation rather

---

1. See Jean-Marie Guéhenno, *La Fin de la démocratie* (Paris: Flammarion, 1993); and Guéhenno, *L'Avenir de la liberté: La démocratie dans la mondialisation* (Paris: Flammarion, 1999).

than from outside pressure. This point too often seems to be overlooked in current Western conceptions or in the way Americans talk about the issue. Thus why go to Warsaw and risk being the skunk at the picnic by seeming to disagree? But Madeleine and Bronislav really insisted, even after I told them the way I saw things, so I decided to go anyway, warning them in advance that I would participate in the discussions but that I would not subscribe to a final declaration.

Moïsi: So what happened?

Védrine: I gave my speech, avoided all polemics, spoke of the history and different stages of democratization, expressed my skepticism about instant democracy, and said what I thought should be done, or not done, to facilitate the rapid emergence and consolidation of democracies. I also spoke of the "democratic disenchantment" (a phrase coined by Jacques Delors) and called on the Western democracies to get their own house in order. I have no regrets about this.

Moïsi: How did people react?

Védrine: Rather well—along the lines of, "thanks for having spoken," "it was very interesting," etc. The only thing that shocked certain Americans and Poles, even though I have given them advance warning, was that I did not endorse the final text. This was because it called for the creation of a Community of Democratic States, whose members would get together—in fact with the State Department—to constitute a pressure group within international organizations on everything having to do with democracy. This was so sweeping. In a way, the objective was to set up a group of "guardians" of democracy as an alternative to international organizations, starting with the UN. I could not accept this.

It's a bit as if I were to organize a conference on progress in Paris and at the end ask each participant to consult with the Quai d'Orsay on any document having something to do with progress.

Moïsi: Why did the other participants agree to sign?

Védrine: They applauded the text! And maybe I took the conference and the subject more seriously than the others. The American press was not unconvinced by my arguments. Coming from the U.S. press about a French foreign minister, this is worth noting. If all this has helped deepen the debate about democratization and how best to contribute to it, then it will have been worthwhile.

Moïsi: Let's turn back to globalization. You underline that the West is the leader of globalization. Isn't that a good thing?

Védrine: Yes, so long as we remember that non-Westerners—the great majority, 5 billion out of 6 billion!—increasingly accept universal values of Western origin but resent the way we claim to impose these values on them, all together. They also resent the way we try to take advantage of their new willingness to accept these values.

Moïsi: Do you apply this same reasoning to international justice?

Védrine: For the same reasons, I would like to see it become truly international, which will be the case when sixty countries have ratified the statutes of the International Criminal Court (ICC). As the year 2000 ended, twenty-seven, including France, had done so. This progress in the fight against impunity is fundamental from the point of view of victims in those countries where the national judicial systems are deficient. But here, too, you have to be careful—political leaders can't just pass the buck. Punishing the guilty and resolving conflicts is not necessarily the same thing.

Moïsi: In this world, what are the main factors of risk and of uncertainty? What are the biggest threats?

Védrine: There are numerous uncertainties, some of which we've talked about: unipolar world or multipolar world?; gradually better regulated or increasingly hegemonic or anarchical world?; etc. Let's talk instead about risks: weakness or disintegration threatens to make states increasingly incapable—even if they cooperate closely—of solving problems and facing up to the development of uncontrollable transnational forces. This is the price you have to pay for the ultraliberalism of the past decade: the libertarian, individualist, and consumerist evolution of the rich societies; the social and political tensions exacerbated by the well-known and growing gap between the increasing wealth of some and the stagnation of others; the increasing cultural uniformity, the flattening out of identities and ways of life; the end of diversity and the ungovernability; and the absence of rules to frame globalization.

But beyond the risks there are threats: the proliferation of weapons of mass destruction, first of all. The fear most often invoked is not so much the proliferation of nuclear weapons held by states—of the approximately 33,000 existing warheads today, fewer than 300 are in the hands of the three de facto nuclear weapons powers (Israel, India, and Pakistan)—but rather the spread of weapons that could be used for nuclear terrorism, or products that could be used to make biological or chemical weapons. Another threat is organized world crime, based on the drug trade. The annual turnover of global crime is estimated to be some $750 billion to $1 trillion, which is more than China's GDP and almost as much as Italy's ($1.157 trillion). The turnover of drug traffic alone is estimated at between $400 and $500 billion, more than that of the oil and gas industry, twice as much as that of the automobile industry, and more than all of Africa's GNP! Finally, there is the terrorism that arises from disorder and injustice and that sooner or later turns into a criminal enterprise. All these threats are the objects of serious and active international cooperation. I put aside what the Americans used to call "rogue states," those that threaten world (or American) order, which are suspected of making weapons of mass destruction and of having hostile intentions toward the West.

Moïsi: Which countries would you consider to be rogue states today?

Védrine: I never used this ostracizing American terminology, which in any case was inconsistently applied. For the United States, the states in question are Iraq, Cuba, Sudan, Iran, Libya and North Korea, though during 2000 the Americans stopped using the phrase "rogue state." The United States justifies its national missile defense project by the North Korean missile threat. Can one seriously think that if that country's leaders were seeking to build up their weapons it was to threaten the Western countries—which have the most formidable arsenal ever built and the capacity for massive retaliation? Some Americans reply to this by suggesting that these countries don't obey "our" rationality. This is what the Americans used to think about the Russians, the French, the Chinese, and others. Of course, even a marginal or hypothetical risk must be taken seriously by governments, as a measure of prudence. Thus so-called dual use exports, which can be used to make weapons of mass destruction, are strictly monitored. We think it necessary to be extremely watchful, but that does not justify upsetting the entire strategic system.

Finally, if the scientists are right, in ecological terms there is a true global threat—global warming—and many specific threats—the lack of potable water, for example. But to respond to such threats, nothing less than a radical revolution in our economy and way of life would be necessary.

Moïsi: There is one global actor, the United States, that is not doing its part in this regard, in the face of this global threat.

Védrine: That's the least one can say. Energy lobbies, the role of the automobile, resistance from public opinion, and American habits of consumption lead the United States to refuse to make the commitments we need. Europe has been more courageous because in 1997, in Kyoto, it committed to reducing its greenhouse gas emissions by 8 percent by 2010. Since a very large share of French electricity is produced by nuclear power, France puts out a lot less greenhouse gases, and France was thus only asked to stabilize its emissions. By contrast, developing countries were asked to cut back by 5.7 percent, the United States by 7 percent, and Japan by 8 percent. Since Kyoto, France is one of the few countries that has more or less upheld its commitments, thanks to its nuclear-generated electricity. Unfortunately, at the November 2000 Hague conference on climate change, the international community was unable to agree how to move forward.

Moïsi: For you, then, globalization brings with it opportunities, but also uncertainties, risks, and threats.

Védrine: Yes, and that's why the French government stresses so strongly that states need to work together to make the most of globalization.

At the UN General Assembly on September 20, 1999, Prime Minister Lionel Jospin thus put forward the idea that, facing the temptation of unilateralism and ultraliberalism, "the more the world globalizes, the more it needs rules." Thus to reinforce the stability of the financial and monetary system and ensure the political legitimacy of the IMF [International Monetary Fund], which is being challenged, we need to "better involve developing countries in the adoption of joint rules and make private financial actors more responsible regarding the consequences of their decisions for countries in crisis." Lionel Jospin also spoke about French proposals on speculative funds and tax havens, as well as a number of other issues that need work: better complementarity among international institutions, responsibility toward the poorest countries (meaning solidarity and fairness), affirmation of common values in the struggle to protect children (against their forced involvement in armed conflict, the sale of children, and child prostitution or pornography), for women's rights, for universal health care, for the application of the precautionary principle regarding the environment and sanitary security. This analysis is what inspires the French government's many initiatives and propositions.

But to manage globalization, responsible and capable governments are necessary. Yet today the five largest global companies have an annual turnover equal to the GNP of 132 of the members of the United Nations. The December agreement on the United States' UN contribution was only made possible by Ted Turner's $35 million contribution. In the global era, who will regulate whom? Who will organize whom? Can we apply basic principles of democracy, like elections, transparency, and responsibility to the global level? These are serious questions.

France in the World

DOMINIQUE MOÏSI: We were just talking about the process of globalization. Does this phenomenon affect France positively or negatively? Are the cards in France's deck well adapted to the process of globalization? Is France more of a good student or a black sheep?

HUBERT VÉDRINE: A good student of which teacher? I don't think in these terms. But let's admit it: globalization does not *automatically* benefit France. Globalization develops according to principles that correspond neither to French tradition nor to French culture: the ultraliberal market economy, mistrust of the state, individualism removed from the republican tradition, the inevitable reinforcement of the universal and "indispensable" role of the United States, common law, the English language, Anglo-Saxon norms, and Protestant—more than Catholic—concepts. Historically, French identity has been defined by and built upon a strong central state, first monarchical, and then republican. It was painstakingly built by jurists and based on the idea that France had a specific political, legal, and cultural role to play in the world. France must thus make an exceptional effort to adapt. And it has already shown itself capable of making this effort! Just watch the films of the 1950s over again to make the comparison. The U.S. ambassador to France during the second Clinton administration, Felix Rohatyn, was right to be surprised by the lack of self-confidence of the French despite the fact that over a period of thirty to forty years this country has undergone a spectacular transformation from a rural country to a big industrial power and created a very dynamic service economy. Our mentalities and our ways of life have changed, but our identity endures. We have to continue to change while remaining ourselves. This is the French government's policy. We are doing so, including in our foreign policy, and in our European policy, which can no longer really be considered "foreign" policy.

MOÏSI: Isn't there also an important question of size? In the era of globalization, it seems it's best to be really big, like the United States, or very small, like Singapore. But France is just medium size.

VÉDRINE: No, it's not a question of size. Size and a big population can also be handicaps. Besides, a lot of small countries are destined to be dependent. France, on the other hand, has a number of useful assets; but there are different ways to take advantage of them. You can't take anything for granted. France cannot rest on its laurels, as if it sits on some sort of Olympic throne where it remains above it all. Nor can it think that all it has to do is express itself—the famous voice of France!—for its desires to be taken as orders to others. Happily, fewer and fewer French people think this way, but this conception endures among some intellectuals. All that constitutes our power, our influence, and our position in today's world, our ideas and our projects, must be defended and enhanced by new, dynamic, and forward-leaning policies and diplomacy.

MOÏSI: Thus no Maginot line but a positively oriented project?

VÉDRINE: Yes, since 1989–91, France has gone about reinventing its foreign policy. The defense of traditional positions remains indispensable, but it is far from sufficient. France's unique position as a Western country that acted like a hinge between East and West disappeared with the bipolar world. You've got to know how to adapt your methods to a transformed world. That's why it has again become important—much more so than twenty years ago—to make the right analyses and forecasts about the new balance of forces, about the new uncertainties and threats, and about what the French want and what they reject. The French government calls for more rules to frame globalization so that it doesn't only come down to a revival of "might makes right." Today, the strongest are the richest and the best informed. The question is who will make the rules? The UN Security Council? The G-8? The World Trade Organization (WTO) or the International Monetary Fund (IMF)? The European Union (EU)? Or will it be the giant multi-national companies, markets, pension funds, and rating agencies? Political leaders or judges? The media, scientists, or engineers? What is clear is that all this requires a foreign policy that is not static, nor defensive, nor merely declaratory. Nor can it be arrogant, since you need allies—who may vary depending on the subjects and the projects you're trying to accomplish—to constitute blocking minorities or consensus. You need a policy that's clear, creative, and flexible.

You spoke about a Maginot line. Let's not use this simplistic and disparaging reference to our cultural policies. Even in the spirit of open competition there are emerging activities that must be protected lest they never have a chance to succeed. For cultural products, protection is justified in two ways: by their impact on the language, the mentality, and the deep identity of the country; and by the quasi-monopolistic position that American cultural industries have won for themselves, thanks to a vitality and creativity that we all acknowledge and admire. But that does not mean that we have to agree to be swallowed up by a tidal wave! When competition is too unequal, protection is justified as a way of giving things a chance to grow. But purely legal protections may not suffice if technological progress allows people to get around them.

Moïsi: The very idea of devoting a whole section of our discussion to culture, to the impact of culture on foreign policy, and to the role that culture can play in the definition and application of foreign policy, is quite French. I doubt such a set of questions would come up in any other European country—or anywhere else, for that matter. How do you explain this unique situation?

VÉDRINE: I would explain it through history. In most other countries, either the culture and language of the country had no real global resonance, or the culture did play a role abroad but without any particular support from the state. In these countries, no one would ever think of asking the foreign minister about these matters, because he would have no particular means or competence to do anything about them. And for most of these countries, the idea of a global cultural role would not be an issue anyway. Obviously this is not the case for the United States, but there it's the chief executive officers of America Online (AOL), Disney, or CNN whom you'd have to talk to. When AOL took over Time-Warner, the *Washington Post* wrote that this was going to further reinforce American cultural domination of the world, and that any resistance would be in vain. At least they were honest!

France is a particular case. First, because of its language—originally determined by a royal decree by François I in Villers-Cotterets in 1539—which for about 150 years, from the late eighteenth to the early twentieth century, was the language of royal courts and European elites, and thus also the language of international relations. It has remained for a long time the language of treaties. That's how French acquired a universal dimension and prestige that it retains, in part, today.

Moïsi: But in many ways the twentieth century has seen the defeat of the French language. In 1914 almost all the chancelleries of the world communicated in French. In 2000 the global language of communication is English, in its American version. Yet language is the key tool for promoting one's civilization and culture.

VÉDRINE: Defeat is too strong a word, but let's not deny the facts. Let's try to be realistic without being masochistic. It is true that French has lost its status as the sole language of chancelleries and as the language of international relations. Let's not forget, in this context, that it was Clemenceau who accepted English—which he spoke fluently—as the second official language of the Treaty of Versailles. This phenomenon has been reinforced throughout the twentieth century; it accelerated after World War II, and even more after the fall of the Berlin Wall. But we don't need to pile on with excessive nostalgia or defeatism! First, the whole world didn't speak French; beyond the French-speaking world it was only the elites, about 1 percent of the populations of the important countries of that era. The world did not go from French to the sort of American jargon now spoken by everyone who communicates in a globalized world, leaving pure Oxford English behind in the process!

Should French be defended? Yes! Absolutely! I don't accept the idea that it would somehow be "old fashioned" to defend our language. A lot of French élites reject this defense of our language on the grounds that it has sometimes taken too pure a form or been too bureaucratic or chauvinistic. But it remains vital for our identity. The result is strange: whereas the Spanish have no qualms about promoting their language, which in any case is very dynamic, and the Germans also have no qualms about it—look at their growing demands within Europe—and the Chinese and the Russians and the Arabs also do it, the French, terrorized by the image of the French beret and the baguette, are now shying away! This would make French the only major language of communication and culture that, while admittedly supported by active public policy, would be the object of indifference and embarrassed silence among France's own élites! These people who think they are so clever and make fun of "backward" laws and "paper barriers"—and who dream only of melting into the global village—are mistaken. They're nothing more than froth and risk provoking a violent backlash from an identity under threat.

Moïsi: But what does it mean to defend your language?

Védrine: Doing everything so that people today have the desire or the need to learn, to understand, to read, and to speak French. This action must be based on realism. Thus it would be counterproductive to demand that French culture only be expressed in French. In the instructions I gave to the Department of International Cooperation and Development (DGCID), I asked them to stop rejecting foreign students in France who don't yet speak French, so long as they're motivated. Regarding TV5 (a state-sponsored French international station that broadcasts worldwide), I requested that we agree to subtitle or dub our films.

Francophones must be at the same time combative and as dynamic as, say, the Spanish speakers in the United States and also very flexible in the application of this policy. The goal must be to come out of this dilemma on the high road—with a mix of openness (we have to learn several languages), pragmatism (we must translate and dub works in French as much as necessary), and resolution (we must defend and promote our language without complexes, everywhere, including in the United States and in Europe). A lot of people in the world still want to learn French, as they do other languages, and I have the impression that the fear of uniformity is going to reinforce this need for diversity, and thus, among other things, reinforce the need for French. Still, we must of course give non-Francophones good reasons, and the means, to learn French today.

Moïsi: Put another way, no new Toubon law, since this type of measure can be too exclusively defensive?[1]

Védrine: On balance, I actually think there's more to be said for the Toubon law, notwithstanding its shortcomings, than against it, at least compared to the reactions that it provoked. Of course, you can go too far, and there are some things that don't work, but failing to comprehend that language is like a sort of genetic code is something I really don't understand! All the more so in the sense that what is at stake here is not only the adaptation of our language or its enrichment by foreign words, which is a part of life, but a multifaceted threat—change or retreat—that demands a reaction! This reaction, of course, should be forward looking.

Moïsi: Concretely, is the Francophonie a realistic and effective tool for French foreign policy?[2] Seen from abroad, particularly from the Anglo-Saxon world, this rather heterogeneous mix of countries, some of whom speak little or no French, doesn't make much sense. Take the case of Vietnam: frankly, the new Vietnamese élites speak less and less French.

1. The question refers to a 1994 law named after then culture minister Jacques Toubon, imposing fines and even possible jail sentences on those who violated regulations requiring the use of French for advertising, media, scientific conferences, and other aspects of French life.

2. The International Organization of the Francophonie was set up in 1986 to promote the use of French and cultural diversity around the world. It currently has fifty-five members and holds regular summit meetings.

VÉDRINE: Obviously, the Francophonie as an organization can be improved, but I would note that the new resistance to uniformity has given it a boost. The Anglo-Saxon world, since you bring it up, has often found it difficult to understand things that are foreign to it. But that's not the issue. When François Mitterrand organized the first Francophonie summit in 1986, he was not so naïve as to think that the entire populations of the countries involved would speak French. On the contrary, the idea was to take action based on a clearheaded obser-vation about the decline of our language. The Francophonie is a hetero-geneous grouping. So what? Is that not the case for all such large organizations, including the Commonwealth? Does this not constitute the richness of such groups? Why should we only make fun of the Francophonie and not the Commonwealth, or even the "United" Nations, which are not really all that united? And don't the Spanish take advantage of their relations with Spanish speakers without having a complex about it? Why should something that is merely one factor of influence among others be understandable and acceptable for other countries but ridiculous for France? With its fifty-five members and nine candidate members, the Francophonie movement stands forth as an expression of the rejection of cultural and linguistic uniformity. The relations among its members are strengthened by this.

MOÏSI: You've talked about the role of language and the fact that we should not be ashamed of using the links that are created by our lan-guage. Beyond this, can French culture be an instrument—or even a weapon—of our foreign policy?

VÉDRINE: While we do promote its diffusion, French culture exists in its own right; it doesn't belong to the French state and is not a tool. In 1920 the Service des oeuvres (an agency to promote French works of art abroad) was created within the Quai d'Orsay, under the direction of Jean Giraudoux, and it was around this time that the Association française d'action artistique (AFAA) was founded. Culture is not a weapon but an asset for France, and not only for the French foreign minister. When Chinese president Jiang Zemin speaks about Victor Hugo, when Brazilian president Fernando Henrique Cardoso speaks nostalgically about his French teachers or a newly discovered work by Rousseau that he just read, when an Egyptian minister states that the few years of the French presence had more of an impact on his country than eighty years of the British presence, or when you realize that France is the top tourist destination of the world and that French museums are never empty—when you look at all this, how can you not see the impact and the influence of our history, which surrounds us, serves us, and gives us responsibilities all at the same time? This remains the case in a large number of countries, including some that one might have expected to be swamped by Hollywood's output. There are so many names from French literature, art, and culture that have not been extinguished but still resonate much more than disillusioned or hung-up French people think. And I could give contemporary examples in areas like dance, cinema, literature, street art, etc. Here, too, the French people's internalization of their "decline" is excessive and not a good basis on which to make decisions or actions. It's as if they still link it to their nostalgia for a Napoleonic France, compared with which no secondary role for their country would be acceptable.

The link with foreign policy is neither immediate nor direct but indirect, and its long-term effect is very powerful. Still, what you need is a foreign policy that does all it can to nourish this vitality. This is what we're doing with our 155 cultural centers in 88 countries, our 267 educational establishments which have 6,000 students—both French and foreign—and with the 406 million francs that we spend on policies to promote cultural and artistic cooperation, books, and audiovisuals.

The question of international commercial negotiations is important in this regard. Can cultural goods be treated, produced, exchanged, and sold like others? We say no, and we ask that an exception be made for culture. But the "cultural exception" is nothing more than a negotiating technique, a measure of protection. Outside France the expression itself, and the attitude it suggests, have a defensive connotation: nothing to win people's support. I realized this a few years ago while talking with Rosario Green, then the Mexican foreign minister. She was the one who told me, "No one understands this business of 'exception.' If you talked about *diversity* it would have a lot more resonance." And in this area, in particular, we absolutely need allies. What's our real objective? It's the preservation of the cultural identities of the whole world, and thus of global diversity. The Americans worry about monopoly situations when competition is distorted in their own market—look at the

Microsoft case. Well, the United States is on its way to becoming a global Microsoft when it comes to the mass culture business, especially in the area of film. We have a major dispute with the United States over culture and cultural production, in the WTO, the OECD (Organization for Economic Cooperation and Development), and regarding the EU candidate countries. What is certain is that global cultural diversity is a big issue that goes well beyond the question of French language and culture. It is sure to be one of the big debates of the future.

Moïsi: What's unique about France in this area is most of all the relationship between culture and the state, which has no equivalent, as least not since Louis XIV.

Védrine: Indeed, he was the first and the greatest French minister of culture our country has known!

Moïsi: This culture, largely based on the centrality of the state, is a key component of our national and international identity. When you introduce yourself as French while abroad, you're seen as an heir of Molière, Pascal . . .

Védrine: . . . and Balzac, Zola, Proust, Sartre, Camus, Foucault, Derrida, and so many others. It's a legacy of history. But it's not a product of diplomatic decisions. It was not the centrality of the state that made the global reputations of these figures, it was their own genius. History gave us this legacy, and making sure this legacy lives is part of the responsibility of a foreign minister. As a day-to-day matter, however, where foreign policy is concerned, this is more a background issue than a tool.

Moïsi: But if the elites that are being trained in African or Latin American countries no longer have Pascal or Sartre as reference points, but instead purely Anglo-Saxon models, since they're mainly doing their advanced studies in U.S. universities, this specificity will disappear, and leaders who still use French culture and civilization as a reference point will become a species in the process of extinction?

Védrine: That's exactly right, and this, too, requires action. Beyond the questions of language and culture, the issue of education is extremely important for our influence in fifteen or twenty years. That's why Claude Allègre—then education minister—and I, in the summer of 1998, decided to modify and give a boost to the promotion and presentation of French higher education all over the world. We became conscious of the fact that over the course of a decade or two, the flows of students had completely reversed, and that the children of élites around the world were no longer educated anywhere except the United States—or in a few rare countries that had a particularly active policy to attract students, such as Australia, which invites a lot of Asians to do part of their university work there. The United Kingdom has also lost a lot of ground to the United States in this area, which proves that it's not a language problem. Large numbers of students still come to study in France, but only from Africa or North Africa, which is not enough. A blindly restrictive visa policy was making this problem even worse, so then interior minister Jean-Pierre Chevènement and I went about fixing it. This is also why Claude Allègre and I created an agency called Edufrance, which brings together and coordinates the supply of educational opportunities from all the universities and Grandes Ecoles on the market. I use the word "market" deliberately, because people are prepared to pay for a quality education. The result has been spectacular: all it took was for Edufrance to start working with Mexico, New Delhi, and Cairo and demand took off. Students from around the world are thirsty for modernity; they're fascinated by America, but they're also smitten by something else: diversity; and consequently, if we know how to offer it to them, France.

Moïsi: Is that true in all disciplines?

Védrine: It remains true, to a greater or lesser degree, in a number of disciplines. But there's one area where our prestige remains particularly strong: law. There, too, throughout the world, I meet leaders who speak to me with emotion about their French professors. Obviously, Anglo-Saxon law—"common law"—is penetrating everywhere, pulled along by globalization, business law, and the big Anglo-Saxon law firms (the "Big Five"). But our civil law, with its Roman-Germanic origins, is resisting, notably within Europe. It is, after all, extraordinarily well adapted for a number of things, like government concessions for public utilities, and we all know how good our water and utilities services are. There, too, it is essential for diversity to be preserved. This is urgent.

Moïsi: In this area, as with culture, this is true if we can manage to combine traditions, diversity, and modernity. Just so long as we don't become a museum of French history!

Védrine: We are managing to do this and will continue to do so. I am confident about this. History and a strong identity are also assets. But you're right, where culture is concerned we also have to avoid giving the impression that all we're doing is trying to keep a fading star from burning out completely. Our heritage remains prestigious. When we add to that French culture today, people are even more interested. This is spectacular in the area of contemporary dance. And, even if it seems unrelated, look at the prestige Paris has won back in the area of architecture over the past twenty years. It began in the late 1970s with Beaubourg, the Musée d'Orsay, and the Institut du Monde Arabe. It became even more clear with the major projects undertaken by François Mitterrand—the most important of which was the fantastic job done by I. M. Pei with the Louvre. And it goes on under Jacques Chirac with the Musée des Arts Premiers. Paris has not only become the most visited city in the world by tourists, but a required stop for architects from around the world. The same thing applies to the issue of language: beyond some vague cultural attraction, you've got to give people *current* reasons to learn French.

Moïsi: Isn't the new LVMH building in New York, designed by Christian de Portzamparc, a good example of what we're talking about? Isn't this sort of a counterpart to I. M. Pei's pyramid in Paris?

Védrine: Indeed. Architects from China, Denmark, England, Chile and many others have been able to build in Paris. There are today a lot of great French names in international architecture: Jean Nouvel (Fondation Cartier, Galeries-Lafayette in Berlin), Christian de Portzamparc (Cité de la Musique, French embassy in Berlin), Dominique Perrault, Jean-Michel Wilmotte, and many others.

Moïsi: After this partial inventory of France's assets, let's ask what France can offer the rest of the world. What is now unique or profoundly original about our message, our method, or our approach? Does this question make sense any more, or is it nothing but a reflection of anachronistic arrogance?

VÉDRINE: This question is far from arrogant. On the contrary, it's a reflection of an existential uncertainty that has no basis. It gives the impression that France needs to justify itself, that it can only get others to recognize that it still exists by proving that it is still useful. But who is to judge this? This is unacceptable. France *exists*, plain and simple, just like Germany, Japan, Russia, Great Britain, the United States, and the others.

MOÏSI: Let me rephrase my question. France is the only country, along with the United States, that sees itself as bearing a universal message. What, in the day-to-day reality of French foreign policy, justifies this pretension? If you accept that history always takes place "on the margins," what is—on the margins of the margins, so to speak—France's contribution today?

VÉDRINE: Never having been one to overuse the rhetoric of the "universal message," I don't feel I have to justify it. But to respond simply to your question about our contribution, the answer is all our proposals to civilize globalization, some of which I have already mentioned.

As for the margins, ours are the same as those of any large country in an era of globalization. I think we manage to expand our influence with an active, flexible foreign policy, both bilateral and multilateral, and also by taking advantage of the leverage Europe offers. Ours is a diplomacy of proposals—when we have ideas that we think will be useful for the rest of the world, we let them be known and try to get them accepted. Otherwise—and I tell the French public this—let's stop letting this notion of "the voice of France" go to our heads, for it manages only to disappoint and irritate at the same time.

MOÏSI: Let me come back to my last point. What, more specifically, are France's assets, and beyond that, those of Europe, which are not exactly the same? What exactly do we have to offer to the world in an age of globalization?

VÉDRINE: This sounds like a question that an American chief executive officer at Davos would ask: does your tax system offer us more than that of your neighbor? What do you have to offer us? Put that way your question somewhat takes me aback. Who is supposed to judge what we have to offer—Davos? The New York Stock Exchange? Pension funds? The U.S. Congress? The Scandinavian Nobel Prize committee? The French, for their part, are asking themselves what globalization has to offer *them*.

France exists, I repeat, and it does not have to justify its existence. What it has to offer comes on top of that. France's assets are not whatever makes it look good, but rather the desire of French people to stand together, which permits them to defend their interests and have their views heard. As for Europe, its assets consist of its economic and demographic weight, its historical success in getting beyond nationalism, its social balance, its diversity, its original institutions so long as they prove capable of reform, and in particular its future, which the entire world is taking note of, and which we're working on.

Moïsi: All well and good. But can these assets be used as in the past?

Védrine: Of course not, but France has very good cards in its deck, so long as it proves able to keep changing its behavior. For me, that's the key. To put it briefly, France's population and territory are only of average size compared to the biggest countries out there, but France is very homogeneous. It's a country that, largely because of its history, continues to exercise considerable influence around the world, but which is still very dynamic. It's a country that over the past twenty years or so has succeeded in achieving economic and social changes that place it, depending on what criteria you use, in fourth or fifth place out of 189 countries, which is pretty good. It's a country whose leading companies are now among the best in the world, which has managed to transform its agricultural sector into an ultramodern instrument of production and export, whose technologies are among the most advanced, whose social policy remains extraordinarily generous, and which, for the last four years, has managed to reduce unemployment, now below the threshold of 10 percent. It is a country that fascinates and attracts others—as I already mentioned, with over 70 million visitors per year, it is the most visited in the world. It is a country with particular political capabilities to lead, with a top-flight administration and diplomatic service.

Moïsi: But does France still have a universal message?

Védrine: Yes, our conception of globalization. In a world where you have to make alliances and build majorities, it's impossible to impose your ideas solely by proclamation—by the "voice of France" alone—even if there are in fact times when France must raise its voice to stand up for itself. Thus we've had to change our mentality and the way we go about things. We have to keep defending our vital interests just as before; we can say no, alone, to anything that may be unacceptable. This is the meaning of our deterrent force, the ultimate guarantee; and of the Luxembourg Compromise within the European Union, which is still valid; and of the use of our right to speak our minds. On the other hand, to get our ideas accepted, to reach new objectives—such as European defense, new international economic and financial rules, the fight against corruption, the advancement of peace in the Middle East—we can't act alone, by statements or decrees. To succeed, you've got to be capable of convincing others, of leading and forming coalitions to build majorities who agree with you or blocking minorities. This requires a certain way of acting toward others that is antithetical to some of our national reflexes, be they chauvinistic or even universalistic. And you have to agree to work with the United States, which is involved everywhere, without getting hung up about it.

Thus we couldn't keep acting like a great power that thinks its job is to pass on its "message" to others. That remains true in certain important cases. But we've got to be careful lest our European partners end up saying that if by chance the French were to find themselves in the same position as the Americans today, they'd be even more unbearable than the Americans! Many Europeans think this already.

Moïsi: What you're really saying is that to have more influence we've got to act less independently.

Védrine: Not really, since to have influence you've got to be capable of having your own ideas. What sort of influence would the French or Europeans have if all they did was repeat the "politically correct" language of the moment or whatever the current consensus was? Having more influence means adding value to the debate. Not only is independence of mind possible, it's indispensable. Of course you've got to act as required by international relations today: be concrete, simple, and direct; know how to work together; listen to others, don't show off. So long as these conditions are met, France can take advantage of its many assets, including its own cultural "soft power," which it consistently underestimates. On the other hand, if we made a habit of doing things that don't make sense—along the lines of opposing the WTO because it's the Trojan horse of the Americans, even though it was the Europeans who for decades called for such a framework to define the rules of the game—then we would find it hard to defend our interests!

Moïsi: To sum up, for a country of its size, France has some remarkable talents, some assets that result from its history and national will, and the French have got to do their best with them by emphasizing a positive message rather than a closed attitude.

Védrine: That's right. But France must not have any qualms about defending its interests just as any other country in the world would. Indeed, that's the primary mission of our foreign policy. We've got to take responsibility for it. France does this every day in the European Union and in all the other forums for negotiation. But here too, let me repeat, it depends how you do it. Just because France has a vision of the world, of democratization, of development and regulation, does not mean it does not have the right and even the duty to defend its interests. There is no contradiction between defending our vision and our interests.

Moïsi: That requires a certain modesty in the presentation of the defense of our interests. Are we capable of this?

Védrine: There are all sorts of reasons to be proud of our country, and, rather than speaking of modesty, I'd speak of simplicity. Let's take care, as French people, to avoid the arrogance that we're sometimes criticized for—sometimes without good reason, though not always. Let's not go around acting like the "Great Nation" that the German-language press always makes fun of. France is no longer an empire, and it should not mistake itself for a hyperpower. Still, France is a great country, and there is no reason for the French to underestimate themselves either. France is almost always a major player, as you can see when you consider just about any of the big global issues. We've just got to find the right tone.

MOÏSI: Thus a clear and positive project, presented in a simple concrete manner, without arrogance, without a defensive or paranoid attitude . . .

VÉDRINE: . . . and with ambition and a bit more confidence in ourselves. For decades now, the French have been answering yes to the question of whether they think France's influence in the world is declining. If that were really the case we'd have no influence left at all! But do you think we've got less influence now than in 1940, or at the time of the fall of Dien Bien Phu, or the Algerian War?

MOÏSI: There's one aspect of international civil society that we've hardly touched on, which is the role of the media. How can the French foreign minister deal with the growing role of the media—in a time of globalization and CNN—without becoming a sort of prisoner, but rather by using the media in a positive manner? In what way is your role different from that of, say, de Gaulle's foreign minister, Maurice Couve de Murville, forty years ago?

VÉDRINE: It's obvious the media plays a great role. Their power and ubiquity and their ability to send information around the world in real time are the result of technical innovations and geopolitical changes that have torn down political walls. This phenomenon has developed exponentially over the past twenty or thirty years. Think about the fact that every French person over fifteen years old spends nearly four hours a day in front of the television and that there are already nearly 120 channels in France. In Europe there are 700 channels, and in the world at large there are over 5,000! This technological revolution has not failed to influence foreign policy. Public opinion, whether judged by polls or TV ratings, increasingly influences the conception and application of foreign policy in a number of countries. Let's not talk about "opinion-based democracy," which would be disingenuous, but rather about "opinion-driven regimes," or "media-driven systems." This is a reality that we've got to acknowledge, without being obliged to either applaud or condemn it. In the most rich and powerful countries, which are also those where the media play the biggest role, public opinion is subjected to continual bombardment of information with a high emotional content—to attract viewers. This sometimes triggers chain reactions, like storms, set off by the real time media! We all know this is how it now works. In this context, political leaders are like navigators in the face of uncertain winds. A government is not working seriously if it doesn't take these factors into account, but at the same time it couldn't do anything if it just acted like a weathervane. Should we leave it up to the wind to provide direction? I don't think so. All the less so because public opinion forms instant reactions, and it can neither set a long-term course nor choose among powerful, competing, and sometimes contradictory alternatives (except, of course, when it comes to voting). This is the daily role of political leaders.

MOÏSI: Yes, but at the same time, because of the media we're seeing the emergence of what one might rather ambitiously call an "international civil society," which has become an actor in international life that we can no longer ignore.

VÉDRINE: We have spoken about this already. International civil society, in the positive sense of the term, is not only made up of the media, though you're right to emphasize their role.

The global audiovisual media today do indeed have unprecedented power to transmit their message and to influence. We know that watching or listening call upon the same parts of the brain that reading does. Everything happening in real time, as the events themselves are taking place, can really bring emotions to a boiling point. And let's not forget that the media are economic entities, not philanthropic societies or public schools. They've got to make a profit, within the limits of their own value systems, each one obliged to fight to preserve or expand its market share. In this ultracompetitive economy, every radio or television station is in a constant struggle with its competitors. Experienced professionals in the field know the exact reactions—loyalty or channel hopping—that might result from the use of any particular word, image, title, newscaster, order of the subjects, use of live broadcasts, whatever. The big modern media organizations have really gotten a handle on these things.

The international media draw on the numerous events that take place every day in the world to find anything that might be able to grab viewers who are already saturated by images and sought after by dozens of other stations. That's their objective: to prevent the viewer from looking elsewhere by "grabbing them by the gut," as the French writer Julien Gracq put it already fifty years ago, referring to literature that he saw as too politically engaged or simplistic, but which in retrospect is quite rigorous if you consider the role TV ratings play today! Instant images, instant opinion polls—it's as if we're being cooked in a pressure cooker! Again, it's obviously impossible to avoid this completely, but this system doesn't give us any long-term guidance. There are some things you've got to do even if the wind is blowing in the other direction, especially in diplomacy, which is a long-term project.

You referred to Maurice Couve de Murville. Aside from the only TV channel France had then—the embryonic ORTF—was this world very different from the time of Richelieu? The change, and it was a radical one, came later. In any case, in the world today political leaders are obliged to explain themselves constantly. This is indispensable if you want to win support. The problem is that whether you speak out or remain silent, you run the risk either of damaging misunderstandings or of a total failure to communicate. Of course, that then leads you to modify your course of action, since you can't stand up against the views of the majority in too many areas at once. Bowing to the majority can help you to avoid big mistakes, but it also puts a damper on courageous action. The emergence of global opinion constitutes progress in that it reduces ignorance, misunderstanding, fear, and hatred. But that's not enough for the current system to be considered perfect.

Moïsi: This means that beyond his talents as a negotiator, the foreign minister has got to be a communicator—a teacher who must systematically give some order to the facts and explain the reasoning behind what he does. His role is to teach public opinion to distinguish between the trend and the trendy.

Védrine: This is a good summary. And by the way, it is true of all ministers in a government, not least of the prime minister himself. After all, sometimes a certain choice of words doesn't go over well. While the war in Chechnya was raging, without supporting Chechen independence, I said that this conflict was of a "colonial" nature. The Russians didn't take very well to this! On February 7, 2000, in Moscow, Vladimir Putin, at the time interim president, criticized me personally for this. In Paris, my comments came across as strong but accurate. During the same trip, after having been seen by Mr. Putin, I said I found him to be intelligent, quick, committed to Russia's status, determined to stop the decline of his homeland, and therefore a "patriot." Madeleine Albright, by the way, had already said this. Some in Paris criticized my use of this term, alleging it to be indulgent! Yet it is undebatable that Mr. Putin is a Russian patriot, not a Chechen one. Maybe I should have said "nationalist"! I suppose people have forgotten that, according to Rousseau, to be a patriot is to be "tough on foreigners." Bill Clinton, Tony Blair and fifteen others have since showered more praise on Mr. Putin than I did.

In any case, a foreign minister must not only act but also help others to understand what he's doing and why he's doing it. He must also explain what the French president of the republic and prime minister are doing. He's got to respond to the curiosity, the questions, and even the concerns of public opinion, to be ready to provide the public on a regular basis with a framework for understanding what he's doing. Any given policy is all the more powerful and wins more support abroad if it is known to reflect a consensus at home.

Moïsi: Since you've been in office, have there been any cases where you would be justified in saying that the press really did a terrible job, unjustifiably complicating French foreign policy decisions? And on the contrary, any cases where you would say that the press was particularly helpful, an ally, so to speak?

Védrine: Both types of case are present all the time. I'd describe it as constant pressure. Every day the press generates illuminating reports, new information, original analyses, and sometimes even useful ideas and directions, even if they weren't initially put forth as such. I read the press extensively myself. But when you say to a journalist, "You criticize, but what are you proposing?" they respond, "That's not my job." Even editorialists do this. But at the same time, the press too often dramatizes and simplifies the analysis, compares things that don't bear comparison, has no memory, has a short-term bias, editorializes like mad, and has no qualms about going after people. In the popular press you have headlines like "The Salaries of Top Management!" or "Polluted Beaches!" to get attention. In the diplomatic area what you get is "The

Moral Imperative!" or "The Duty to Intervene!" or "France's Helpless-ness!" or "Europe's Silence!" or "the UN Fiasco!" (if not the opposite in each case). What are these commentaries and this automatic indigna-tion based on? On the assumption, dominant since the fall of the Berlin Wall, that the Western world, with its "values," must and can dominate the world of the "third millennium," to use just some of the hyperbole. Even if you have to take it into account, this simplistic presentation of things in no way helps public opinion understand either the complexity or the reality of the world.

Another failing of the media is that, under the pretext of trying to avoid double standards, they treat everything the same way (Kosovo, East Timor, and Chechnya) and they put forward the same remedies (political intervention, sanctions, armed intervention) no matter what the situation. You'd never see this type of logic accepted in the field of medicine! It's true that a lot of political leaders give out rope to hang themselves with, by constantly talking about the "consistency" of their actions—which is understood as their standardization, whereas it's their pertinence and effectiveness that should be most important—or by evoking morality, implying that the choice was between a moral solution and an immoral one!

Moïsi: So you find a pragmatic, case-by-case approach to be more subtle and sophisticated than the simple approach of well-intentioned moralists.

Védrine: The advantage of this pragmatism is that it's more effective, so long as you keep within general principles, of course.

Moïsi: More general than generous, one might say. Let's move from the press and media to public opinion. In the United States, the chal-lenge leaders face is to overcome the natural indifference of a people who, sheltered by their geography and their power, feel self-sufficient. In France, you don't get the impression that public opinion is disinter-ested in foreign policy, but rather that, for a large majority of the French, our national identity depends on the implementation of this policy. When you see the French flag flying in some remote corner of the world, or if you look at examples of the influence of French foreign policy, there is a rather positive reaction.

VÉDRINE: That's still true to a certain point. Part of French public opinion does indeed consider that France's special role consists of intervening abroad in the interest of others. This goes way back and is rather specific to France (along with the United States). You could almost say, tongue in cheek, that this goes back to the Crusades and that it has been perpetuated under different forms—monarchical, Napoleonic, secular, republican, military, or intellectual—right up to the present day under the name of the "homeland of human rights." (France has given itself this title despite the fact that the Americans claim to have produced the founding documents in this area earlier or at the same time as France. There is also no reason why Britain should historically have less of a claim to be the homeland of human rights than France.) These policies have been referred to as colonial empire, spreading the faith, spreading democracy, a secular and republican ideal, a mission to civilize, and finally, intervention. This is an appealing aspect of the French character that remains quite strong, and which has inspired and still inspires some magnificent examples of devotion to duty, but is nonetheless problematic.

MOÏSI: Its current incarnation is in the form of "French doctors," the various French medical aid organizations who have made a name for themselves by intervening in humanitarian crises around the world.

VÉDRINE: In the beginning, they—notably Bernard Kouchner—took real risks to save victims who had been abandoned by everyone else. But since then, some of these organizations have drifted toward something like a mix between humanitarianism and the Crusades, a sort of modern hospitaller, with the media thrown in for good measure. This altruism, which mixes true generosity, paternalism, and the conquering instinct, remains in place and is very demanding. You see this clearly when you try to analyze all the expectations there are of French foreign policy. The most basic, classical expectation, which is obviously the basis for what we do, is that foreign policy must guarantee our national security, our autonomy, protect us from threats, and better permit us to defend our interests and our values. But you hardly hear about this in the daily chatter. Maybe it goes without saying? On the other hand, you constantly hear one-dimensional expectations as if France were a specialized organization with a single social goal. Progress toward human rights in other countries, for example, or progress toward European integration—these are noble aspirations on important subjects, but they cannot alone constitute our *entire* foreign policy. You cannot have a foreign policy without looking at the big picture, and you cannot have action without priorities.

It's striking that, whenever there's a crisis, we are called upon to "intervene."

MOÏSI: I intervene, therefore I am?

VÉDRINE: In a way. But to be complete it is necessary to mention two other schools of thought that you find in French public opinion and that are less tempted by interventionism. The first is an attitude of gloomy nostalgia: since we're no longer the France of Napoleon's time, what's the use? Adherents of this school content themselves with denunciations of the Americans or Germans, or sometimes of Europe or globalization. The second school brings together those who think we no longer have the means to act abroad and that we would be better off focusing on improving our own society as an example to others. It's a sort of Scandinavian concept that, in the European Union, is gaining steam. The idea is that Europe would not become a power in its own right, but would simply be a socially and morally exemplary "space." Internationally, it wouldn't worry so much about acting, but would focus on taking the right *positions*. Foreign policy needs to take this way of thinking into account. But it has to be more than that if it is to survive.

MOÏSI: The press doesn't prevent the minister from providing direction, as you said at the beginning of this chapter. The fact that French public opinion is generally favorable to interventionism, subject to the reservations you mentioned, is a rather unique aspect of our foreign policy today, at least if you compare it to the policies of the United States or some other European countries. This gives the French government a rather large margin of maneuver to "provide direction." To be sure, we're starting to see parliamentary commissions being set up to look into the odd African crisis, but this is nothing compared to the U.S. Congress's ability to veto the use of force to prevent the government from providing direction.

VÉDRINE: Committed interventionists will be delighted to hear that French leaders have freer hands than their American counterparts, though the French parliament is in fact becoming more watchful. But this does not therefore give interventions legitimacy or make them advisable. As for the last U.S. Congress, it's true that for years it has waged a sort of guerilla war against the executive branch to make life difficult for President Clinton, not least by blocking for years the payment of America's UN debt. But you couldn't say that these initiatives, if you put them all together, provided any sort of direction. What they do is reflect a philosophy both isolationist and unilateralist (thus the fondness for sanctions, which are so handy), which constrains the administration's pursuit of world leadership and interventionism.

MOÏSI: If you had to draw up a balance sheet of your relations with the media over the past three and a half years, what would it be: generally positive, complicated, or outright negative?

VÉDRINE: It's an exciting relationship, even passionate. Since June 1997, I have tried to explain what France is doing subject by subject, crisis by crisis. I think the media largely understood this, with each individual free to make his or her own judgment. I wouldn't say the same about my concern that states not be further weakened if we want to control globalization, now that the liberal-libertarian-individualist-consumption ideology dominates in the West, where the market economy prevails. It's also not the case with regard to my belief that we've got to proceed differently in relations between the West and the rest of the world if we really want to promote genuine and durable democracy. The West is currently closed to any critical examination of these two points, especially the second one. But in the end I managed to draw some attention to real issues, and the Anglo-Saxon press, most of all, took an interest.

MOÏSI: There's a point we haven't talked about yet, but which is relevant to this part of the discussion—the role of "cohabitation," when the French president comes from a different political party than the rest of the government. Is being a foreign minister in a cohabitation government very different from in a "normal" government?

VÉDRINE: It's different. The foreign minister in this situation can have more authority and means of action so long as he can work in good conditions with the president of the republic and the prime minister. I have always benefited, in doing my job, from the confidence of the prime minister, who selected me and who is known to direct the government I'm in with authority. He applies the full meaning of article 20 of the constitution, including in its European and international dimensions, where he has strong convictions.[3] In the Fifth Republic, the president of the republic traditionally plays an eminent or preeminent role in these areas. I think I can say that I get along well with him. Cohabitation is not an ideal situation, but, when the French people impose it with their vote, you've got to accept that in the interest of the country. I am not, by the way, convinced that holding presidential and legislative elections on the same day would be enough to get the French to choose the same parties in each! But that's a separate matter. What is clear is that the French don't hate this situation.

MOÏSI: Perhaps they have found a balance between these two parts of the executive branch that, under the Fifth Republic, doesn't exist between the legislative and executive branches.

VÉDRINE: Maybe. In any case, you've got to deal with it in ways that cannot be seen to go against the interest of the country. In this "shared domain" between the president of the republic and the government (we all know that the old expression *domaine réservé* was incorrect), you've got to have agreement between both sides not only on the setting of objectives but on their application. This requires a particular willingness on the part of the president, the prime minister, and the government to maintain an open dialogue and to work together in every stage of the process, from the analysis that takes place before a decision all the way through to the implementation stage. It requires that they speak with a single voice. Even more than in a normal single-party or coalition government, this means that there must be constant discussion between the president and the prime minister, the foreign minister, and the

3. Article 20 of the French constitution states that the government "determines and conducts the nation's policy" and "is in charge of administration and of military forces."

defense minister, and between the prime minister and the foreign and defense ministers. It means there must be daily exchanges between the relevant chiefs-of-staff, preparatory meetings before summits, and coordination of position papers. When the spokesperson for the Foreign Ministry speaks in the name of the president and the government, he or she is doing so "in the name of the French authorities." Thanks to this way of doing business, we have managed since June 1997 to develop French positions that never handicapped us on the international stage and that were often admired by others for their coherence. In some cases these positions held up better to challenges—either by events or during negotiations—than the positions of other "normal" governments, which had not been submitted to the same degree of clarification and synthesis beforehand. This may be paradoxical, but it's clear. Look at Europe: Agenda 2000, the European budget for 2000–06, enlargement, and the preparation of the French presidency, the Nice summit. And look, too, at Kosovo, Seattle, the Middle East, Africa, Russia, UN reform, and so much else.

Moïsi: After having initially said that your instinct was to be opposed to cohabitation, you now seem to be coming to a more positive conclusion.

Védrine: I'll just stick with the assessment that we've gotten this situation under control without undermining the interests of the country. I wouldn't extend this observation to other areas beyond those of foreign policy and defense. And I wouldn't extrapolate it either—each cohabitation is different.

Moïsi: We have seen how France needs to act in this context. We'll look later at Europe.

Védrine: The two need to go together.

Moïsi: We'll come back to it. Before turning to the United States, how would you sum up the objectives of French foreign policy?

Védrine: To preserve French vital interests, which are necessary to its security, identity, and prosperity. To take advantage of its margin of maneuver, its influence, and its ingenuity, so that Europe gets stronger without France getting weaker, so that enlargement succeeds, and so that Europe becomes a key world player in the future. To promote rules and preserve the diversity the world needs. To reduce the growing unjust and explosive gaps that exist among countries. To promote solid democratization everywhere. To reach the right balance between the historical experience of reality and the demands of modern ethics. To have what we're doing be understood both by our international partners and by the French.

How to Deal with the United States?

DOMINIQUE MOÏSI: Let's talk about the United States now. Why does globalization seem to be so much in America's benefit? Is that country perfectly endowed with the qualities necessary to succeed in the age of globalization: the sense of initiative, the taste for risk? Isn't America's strength really the result of the triumph of individualism and will? Doesn't it lie in the idea that the individual can make a difference, that he is put on this earth to improve the world he lives in, even if only a tiny bit, "on the margins," so to speak?

HUBERT VÉDRINE: This is indeed how I see what makes up the power of the "American dream." Without forgetting that its inherent individualism did not shield the United States from some very serious crises, you've got to acknowledge that the market economy, market society (unfortunately!), and ever-growing individualism go hand in hand. This has its merits, but it leads to the fragmentation of collective structures. The United States is very much at home in this sort of world. We have seen why. I don't think France is ready to submit to this type of globalization without thoroughly examining it first.

Moïsi: Should the United States be compared with the Roman Empire rather than with the more recent British Empire? And should we conclude that its history is only just getting started?

Védrine: America today is much more than the British Empire and closer to what the Roman Empire was compared to the rest of the world in that era. Maybe not in terms of duration, but surely in terms of universality and influence. And even so, at the borders of the Roman Empire there were barbarians who put up some resistance in the Germanic forests, and other powers beyond the *limes*, like the Parthians and Chinese. But even this is not the case today. American globalism—the "World Company," to use the expression of a spoof on French television—dominates everything everywhere. Not in a harsh, repressive, military form, but in people's heads. This is the "soft power" that you talked about at the beginning of this conversation.

Moïsi: Why are the French so keen on watching American movies?

Védrine: Because these films, initially made profitable in a vast internal market, are backed by huge resources to help them flood markets abroad; because they're well made, with an unmatched sense of pace and with themes, symbols, and myths that speak to people; and because they connect all the more with the general public of the world (particularly young people) because that public has over the decades gotten used to American films and television series. This is an area in which supply has created demand, which is also boosted by the distribution system for films. The desire to preserve cultural diversity in the world is in no way a sign of anti-Americanism, but of antihegemony. It's a rejection of impoverishment. Many Americans refuse to make this distinction. American cinema has been enchanting viewers around the world for nearly a century, and that will continue. This is no reason for others to disappear.

Moïsi: But the resistance is all the more necessary and difficult because we are ourselves Americanized, fascinated by America, and because our relationship with the United States is almost schizophrenic!

VÉDRINE: In the past we would have spoken of alienation. In any event, this fascination is very strong today, for the many reasons I've already noted, and because Bill Clinton proved to be a very gifted, likeable, and agreeable president. Since the fall of the Soviet Union, U.S. influence has derived in large part from a very concrete desire on the part of the former communist countries, for example, in Eastern Europe or the Balkans, to be close to America. It is possible to salute this American vitality and at the same time refuse to disappear oneself. France will share in the adventure of globalization, which will also be marked by France. Our entire foreign policy is built around this idea.

In our relationship with the United States, we must perform a delicate but indispensable balancing act. French foreign policy after 1958 leaned in general toward criticism, and there were plenty of reasons for that! Today, I believe we should be capable of saying yes when it's in our interest to do so, notwithstanding those who gauge our diplomacy according to the sole criterion of how much disagreement it creates with Washington. And I think we should also be able to say no when that's in our interest—when our view of the world is different—without it being a big deal. We should be capable of cooperating with the United States in the Balkans, in the Middle East, in Africa, within the G-7/G-8, wherever we decide to do so. But we should also be able to oppose the United States if necessary. Examples would include the unilateral and excessive laws passed by the Senate to sanction non-American companies that invest in Iran or in Cuba, or the plans that would put the Anti-Ballistic Missile (ABM) Treaty in doubt, or the export of food products chock full of hormones or genetically modified organisms without adequate precautions, etc. That's what it means to be friends that are allied but not aligned.

MOÏSI: Is this easy to do?

VÉDRINE: No, of course not. It requires character, and it makes a permanent dialogue between political leaders on both sides of the Atlantic all the more necessary. In fact, this dialogue was constant between President Clinton, President Chirac, and Prime Minister Jospin, as between Madeleine Albright and myself. Talking to the Americans allowed us, in certain cases, to influence them—look at their evolution on the Middle East—but most of all it reassured the other countries we need—and who would never want to be pulled along by the French in some sort of old-style anti-American guerilla movement. The more our attitude is understood by others, the bigger our margin of maneuver. This dialogue is very important where European defense is concerned, in order to avoid misunderstandings. And there are also cases where the Americans' arguments convinced us.

Moïsi: Do you detect in France the beginnings of a return to the sort of anti-Americanism we saw in the 1960s and 1970s, with the denunciation of globalization having replaced that of imperialism?

Védrine: No, I don't think so, on the contrary. We talked about the French infatuation with American movies. Most of the French supported the joint American-European action in Kosovo. The United States is widely admired in France, notwithstanding some reservations about violence, the death penalty, guns, the role of money, and now, the electoral system. By contrast, I believe the feeling of differences between the French and Americans is stronger than ever; you hear things like, "They're not like us," "Our societies are not at all the same." The idea of a "Euro-Atlantic world," which NATO is so crazy about, has no resonance in France. And the aversion to—if not outright resistance to—hegemony is very strong; it's getting stronger with globalization. As globalization tends to be equated with Americanization, there is inevitably confusion, which leads some watchdogs to jump up and denounce France's anti-Americanism. But that's not what it is!

Moïsi: Is the United States really ready to go from leadership to partnership in its relationship with Europe? When Europe is absent, the Americans denounce its divisions and weakness; when it seems to show some will and gets organized, America gets nervous or even somewhat irritated.

Védrine: Exactly. To be sure, American leaders—presidents and cabinet members—accept the necessity of a strong Europe. They finally took notice in a realistic way of the creation of the euro. In Kosovo, we worked together in the spirit of true partnership. But this relatively open attitude hardly prevails in Congress, which is too unilateralist to embrace it. And America as a whole can see itself only as the leader—the "indispensable nation," as Madeleine Albright puts it. Her successors will not have a different view. When the United States works with others, it always has a hard time resisting the temptation to tell them what to do. Still, we manage to talk about everything: the Balkans, Russia, China, the Middle East, Iraq, Africa, global problems.

Moïsi: On the question of European defense, Washington oscillates between denunciation of our weakness and respect for our growing efforts. How can we strike the right balance between the North Atlantic Treaty Organization (NATO) and the European Union (EU)?

Védrine: This will indeed be the next big test, where America's acceptance of partnership is concerned. They say they're not hostile to European defense so long as it doesn't lead to "decoupling, duplication, or discrimination."

Moïsi: What do you say to that?

Védrine: That no one either wants to or has the means to duplicate defense systems; that the NATO alliance remains the foundation of the collective defense of its members; that decoupling can only come from them—for example, by putting the ABM Treaty in doubt; and that discrimination (of NATO members that are not in the EU) is not what we have in mind, not least because the countries in question will one day enter the EU. Our goal for European defense is logical, serious, and consistent with the Alliance. Thanks to the rapprochement between the British and the French, we are in the process of getting it up and running, step by step, and we did more during 1999 and 2000 than we had done over twenty years of constant dialogue with the United States.

Moïsi: How can you define a European foreign policy when the secret dream of some French people—to build Europe against the United States—is the nightmare of most of our European partners?

Védrine: This contradiction is progressively being overcome. It comes back to what I was saying earlier: being capable of saying yes or no according to the case at hand. I know of no European, even among the most Atlanticist, who is always prepared to say yes to the United States—for example on the question of the Helms-Burton and D'Amato-Kennedy laws, named after the senators who wanted to ban non-American companies from doing business with Cuba, Libya, and Iran; or on the issue of the American Congress's refusal to pay its UN dues—which it finally agreed to do. Nor do I know any Europeans who want to always say no. That leaves some room to elaborate and affirm a true European position without being gratuitous. Instead, Europe needs to stop being afraid to exist.

Moïsi: Doesn't the American missile defense project (national missile defense [NMD]) risk in the long run upsetting the relationship between Europe and the United States by introducing a new element of structural inequality between them and us?

Védrine: Yes, I believe it does. The United States wants to protect itself from the outside world. It's been an American obsession since the very beginning that in their eyes is not incompatible with global leadership. If you accept that American technology can protect the national territory and American people from all external threats—threats that are exaggerated by blockbuster disaster movies and an obsessive political discourse about "rogue states"—the pressure to build such antimissile systems can become irresistible. Especially if enormous industrial and financial interests are pushing in this direction, as they have been since the "Star Wars" era under Ronald Reagan. At the heart of ultraliberalism, there are some real experts at exploiting political decisions, public money, public opinion, and power all at once!

Moïsi: You find no justification for this program other than that of reassuring American citizens by giving them the illusion of better protection in the face of the vagaries of history, with technology replacing geography in the collective American subconscious?

Védrine: In order to be able to intercept—maybe—hypothetical North Korean or Iranian missiles (and they'd really have to be nuts in Pyongyang or Tehran to fire missiles at the United States!), is it necessary to turn the entire strategic system upside down by proclaiming, in a way, that deterrence no longer deters. Is it worth the risk of renewing the arms race? It's hard to understand why the colossal American nuclear arsenal, which deterred the formidable power of the Soviet Union, would no longer work against microscopic—or theoretical— threats! Unless this is all about something else. We can only hope that the United States will feel better protected. As for ourselves, we are not worried: our defense is effective and our goal is not to penetrate eventual American defenses! But the new U.S. administration risks giving its allies the impression of wanting to create unequal security zones. What if it runs up against the Russian refusal to revise the ABM Treaty and against Russia's threat to withdraw from the START I and II nuclear arms reduction treaties and from the ban on nuclear tests? Should it then, to use a well-known American formulation, shrug it off and run the risk of *decoupling* the two sides of the Atlantic, *duplicating* nuclear deterrence, and *discriminating* among allies?

Why create all these problems out of nothing and hand these arguments to the Russians, the Chinese, and others on a platter? We appreciated the fact that President Clinton—who, it is true, was never a very enthusiastic supporter of this project—was able to resist the enormous pressure that was being put on him and defer these decisions. Let us hope that beyond its early categorical declarations of the intention to deploy, the new administration will seriously study the feasibility of this system, which is far from given. Even more important, from our point of view, we hope that the administration will carefully weigh the problematic motivations and potentially unforeseeable strategic consequences of this project.

MOÏSI: Isn't EU enlargement to the center and east of the continent going to reinforce pro-Western sentiments, to the detriment of pro-European ones, in the heart of Europe?

VÉDRINE: It's true that right after the fall of the Berlin Wall these countries cared only about NATO. In fact, they didn't distinguish between the European Union and NATO and dreamed only of Euro-Atlantic integration. This was the period when Vaclav Havel contributed to the very unfortunate failure of the "European Confederation" idea that François Mitterrand proposed on December 31, 1989, and which would in fact have changed all that followed: all Europeans would have been working together within a common European system for ten years by now!

Added to that is central and eastern Europe's fascination with America, especially American movies and television. Still, the twelve candidate countries discover every day a bit more the reality, the attraction, and the originality of the European Union, as well as the primordial importance for them of joining it. This is why they were so happy that there was an agreement at the EU's December 2000 Nice summit.

Moïsi: In the age of globalization, does a specifically European identity exist—in contrast to a specifically Western one?

Védrine: For me, French identity is a given, just like American identity. European identity is a historical and cultural reality that is now in the process of becoming a political one. Western identity? I don't see this as much. The community of values exists but remains vague and includes some real differences (like over the death penalty), and an alliance system is not enough to make for a common identity. A market economy even less so. Finally, democracy does not belong only to the West.

Moïsi: Finally, how do we work with the United States, which is our partner, our ally, our competitor, and our rival simultaneously? Have you personally introduced a different style, substituting "grumpy yes's" with "harmonious no's"?

Védrine: Another nice way of putting it! I have introduced a new and different style. And, yes, we had to change. The French-American dialogue has never been as intense and consistent as it was under the Clinton administration. Even on the sensitive question of missile defense or on the question of Iraq, where we have different views about the utility of the embargo for regional security. In Africa, it's no longer the case that the Americans see only reprehensible francophones and virtuous anglophones. The war in the Great Lakes region of Central Africa put an end to this black-and-white view of things. As a result, we're working together better toward peace in this region. Regarding the Middle East, I don't think we've ever worked so closely together as during the final months of Bill Clinton's presidency; everyone knows this and can see it, even if we each retained our own particular sensitivities. On the Balkans, we continue to work together, and it's going well. Our interests and approaches to the World Trade Organization (WTO) are not identical, but the very point is to have a framework to discuss these things. On the other hand, the Americans don't really share our overall analysis of the state of the world. Nor do they like what I say about hyperpower, even though they eventually came to understand, as I have pointed out, that this expression is descriptive and not aggressive. They also don't like our warnings about the risks of uniformity, nor the critiques of the French president and government about the harm done by unilateralism, nor our objective of a multipolar world. On the whole, divergences and suspicions reappear when we have theoretical discussions, but concrete cooperation is going well.

Moïsi: Did the exceptional conditions of the U.S. presidential election surprise or shock you? In light of their own rather strange recent elections, can the United States continue to give lessons in democracy to the world like they did at the Warsaw summit in June 2000?

Védrine: While 87 percent of Americans still think that their political system is the best of all, and while they accept that the president, once chosen, is the president in everyone's eyes, these developments—and especially the way the problem was finally resolved—left people in a number of countries rather perplexed. The United States will no doubt continue to give lessons in democracy to the world, but these may be less persuasive.

Moïsi: Will a Bush presidency be very different for Europe from what a Gore presidency would have been? The Republicans' internationalism is more defensive, more oriented toward the defense of American national interests than the Wilsonian internationalism of the Democrats. Under Gore, the United States would have wanted to protect the world from itself. Under Bush, on the other hand, it may want to protect itself from the world—as the NMD project suggests. With which form of internationalism do you find yourself most at ease?

Védrine: With a form of internationalism based on legitimate forms of intervention and that is not only expressed by Western superiority or impatience. That is to say, an internationalism ultimately based on Chapter VII of the UN Charter. And let me add that we should seek to make it easier to use this means by having the permanent members of the Security Council show more self-discipline regarding the use of their veto power in the case of humanitarian situations of extreme urgency.

Moïsi: If relations between Bush's America and Europe may be more tense in the area of security, what about in the area of international trade? Can Bush, since he doesn't have to pay as much attention to American trade unions, be an easier trading partner?

Védrine: It's not for me to speculate about the areas of transatlantic relations that will be more or less tense. Europe's positions are clear— those of the EU regarding trade or European defense, those of its main member states regarding the ABM Treaty. Europe will wait to learn more about the true intentions of the new U.S. administration and will pursue its future course accordingly.

Moïsi: We spoke about Europe, but what about France? Over the past few years you developed a particularly close relationship with Madeleine Albright, who often said how much she thought of you. Now that a new administration has come to power in Washington, French-American relations seem more dominated by irritation than by harmonious confidence. Why is this so? The Anglo-Saxon press asks whether Bush is going to make London or Berlin his privileged partner in Europe. Is it normal that it wouldn't even occur to them to mention Paris?

Védrine: It's true that we worked very closely with the past administration. As for what follows, I think the Anglo-Saxon press is anticipating, or speculating, according to its own agenda. At the moment it's premature to speculate about any of this. You can't characterize something that has only just begun to take place! Moreover, the question of privileged partnerships in international relations no longer makes any sense. Today, each state seeks to take maximum advantage of all of its assets without cutting itself off from anyone. Nor do states take into account the reality of the European Union, which is a community. I have no doubt about the role that France will play in transatlantic relations in the coming years and I can only repeat that we will happily cooperate with the Bush administration to resolve the great problems of the world—in particular, global problems—according to the principles that I have discussed.

Moïsi: Finally, how would you respond to those Americans who remain convinced that French foreign policy is based on anti-Americanism?

VÉDRINE: I can't help but observe that certain stereotypes about French foreign policy die hard in the United States. Some analysts seem to think that French policy consists of systematic opposition to the United States in the vain hope of recovering France's past glory. Believe me, that is not our obsession. But what we do is sometimes construed that way. I read quite recently a whole slew of clichés along those lines in no less a prestigious journal than the *New York Review of Books*. You have to wonder what sort of France those Americans who think like this would want to see? Perhaps a France where no one spoke French, which no longer produced any movies, no longer exported food, got rid of all social protection and became a sort of museum or natural park. I'm joking, of course, and I also know that France is appreciated and studied with curiosity and objectivity in the United States. It's the same in France, where the United States is viewed with fascination and interest, yet also at times is judged with stereotypes.

Let me give you just a couple of examples of bias regarding France. Now that we're in the process of building an autonomous defense capability in Europe—initially with the British and now with the other Europeans—we're accused of wanting to undermine the Atlantic Alliance! In fact this will be a tremendous factor for dynamism in the Alliance.

We have also, periodically, been suspected of pursuing commercial objectives in the Middle East on the grounds that we've expressed reservations about the effectiveness of sanctions against Iraq. This is a bizarre accusation for three reasons. First, I imagine that commercial considerations are present in U.S. foreign policy. But I doubt they're the most important factor. Well, the same applies to French foreign policy. And in this particular case they play no role at all. Second, it's hard to see what benefit France could hope to gain from its proposal to impose more stringent controls, more carefully targeted on the Iraqi regime, which opposes them. Finally, the new U.S. administration is now asking itself the same questions France raised a few years ago, without yet being heard.

Anti-French prejudice regarding the Arab-Israeli conflict also endures even though, like the United States, France is only seeking peace. Earlier French ideas, prescient and long rejected, have today become the acknowledged basis for any settlement.

I could give you many more examples. All these insinuations are quite hurtful, and they're not true. That's why I ask our American friends to take a look at the real France of 2001, at the policy of its government, at its economy—whose performance has been hailed by American publications of the highest standards—and to France's real foreign policy. Like that of the United States, it is determined by France's national interests, but also by its vision of Europe and the world, and by ideas and values that we have, for the most part, in common. From these bases, our policy is continually evolving and adapting. If we agree to do away with ulterior motives and prejudices, if we have a common desire for trust and loyalty, the French and the Americans can do a great deal together for themselves and for the world.

France's European Ambition and Its Dilemmas

DOMINIQUE MOÏSI: Where, in your view, are Europe's borders? Can they still be defined in geographical terms alone, or do we need to talk about "frontiers," in the sense of a project?

HUBERT VÉDRINE: Do we have a frontier that can be seen as a project? Yes, it's making Europe into a great power. But that hardly means that we don't have to understand Europe's geographical limits or to set its geopolitical limits. The European Union (EU) is open to European countries that fulfill its conditions for membership: there should be no doubt about this. There are fifteen of us today, and we're negotiating with twelve others: Poland, Estonia, Lithuania, Latvia, Hungary, the Czech Republic, Slovakia, Slovenia, Bulgaria, Romania, Cyprus and Malta. There are about ten other countries that are unquestionably European. Morocco's candidacy was not accepted in 1987 because Morocco is in Africa. Turkey's candidacy was accepted at the end of 1999, in large part because in 1963 the leaders of what was then called the European Community recognized—perhaps without fully weighing the consequences—Turkey's "European vocation." This recognition played a big role in the December 1999 decision, which remains controversial. In Helsinki, the fifteen EU members thus decided to accept Turkey's candidacy without beginning negotiations with Ankara. This decision disappointed the defenders of a narrowly defined European identity. Those who put a lot of emphasis on respect for human rights in Turkey should be reassured by realizing that this candidacy gives us leverage to help the country evolve. But what do we do about Ukraine or Moldova—without getting into more adventurous speculation about Georgia, Armenia, or even Russia? The EU fifteen need to be clearer about this.

Moïsi: What's your sense? Is the EU feeling a sort of identity crisis today because it doesn't really know where its geography ends?

Védrine: For a long time we didn't have to worry about this. Today, the ambiguity is making people uncomfortable. The response must be geographical, corrected in part by geopolitics. Russia is not asking to join but instead wants to become a major power again. Besides, Russia's joining would destroy the whole European project. For Ukraine, I would prefer to see a status of associated strategic partner. And the same for Turkey, in case we're unable to begin or conclude the membership negotiations. I don't say this because Turkey is a Muslim country that could never enter this "Christian club;" Albania is a Muslim country and a European country at the same time. But looking at it the other way, just because the European Union is *also* a community of values that is building on what it has already accomplished, that doesn't mean that any democratic country from anywhere can join. In that case, why not Japan or South Korea?

Moïsi: How can we conclude this debate? For the time being it seems that the fear of dilution is stronger than any other consideration.

Védrine: I wouldn't say that. It's about time we started paying close attention to the consequences of this major enlargement, if we want it to work. Above all, the European Union has got to maintain control over this process. When the United States announces that this or that country—the Baltic States, Turkey, or any other—must be allowed to join the European Union, and when—as if by chance—it does so on the eve of a European Council of Ministers meeting, I think the Americans are going too far. It's as if the Europeans were to claim to be able to decide when and to which Latin American countries the North-American Free Trade Agreement (NAFTA) should be extended! The history of the twentieth century has left the United States engaged in Europe, where it constitutes the backbone of the North Altantic Treaty Organization (NATO). This does not give it the rights of a sixteenth member of the EU, even if it is often present either in person or in spirit! In addition, enlargement has to be managed and controlled in a way that strengthens the union and does not paralyze it. Thankfully, in Helsinki in December 1999, after ten years, we finally defined a strategy to make enlargement succeed and avoided just letting ourselves slide along as if we were on a sled. And we'll stick to this strategy. The negotiations are serious.

Moïsi: When Europe expresses itself with a single voice, it can stand up to the United States. This was the case with Leon Brittan during the Uruguay negotiations on the General Agreement on Tariffs and Trade (GATT), with Pascal Lamy at the Seattle World Trade Organization (WTO) summit. When it comes to security policy, Europe had always been divided. Today, however, the evolution of France's relations with NATO, Britain's relations with Europe, and Germany's relations with itself are allowing the union to speak with a single voice in this area, too. This helps it not so much to resist America—it's not a question here of resisting—but to appear a credible partner.

Védrine: Speaking with a single voice is a general objective. In the area of defense and security policy, Europe is already in the process of acting as one. What started in summer 1998 with the statements by Tony Blair, Jacques Chirac, and Lionel Jospin became more concrete at the Franco-British Saint-Malo summit and continued within the EU at the Cologne summit. This was in part thanks to the "Kosovo effect," which was felt by more than just the French. From Cologne to Nice, in December 2000, things progressed even more. European defense is in the process of evolving from a chimera to a reality. I think the Europeans will end up imposing themselves as partners on a United States that will initially be reticent, but at the end of the day will be realistic.

Moïsi: Isn't what we are seeing—at least in part—on one hand, the result of greater realism on the part of France, which has taken account of an inevitable security role for NATO, and on the other hand, the beginning of frustration among other Europeans with the way the United States too often behaves?

Védrine: France's realism in this area consists of taking into account all the other Europeans' attachment to NATO; Britain's realism consists of taking into account the stage of development at which the European Union has arrived. It's also clear that the frustration the other Europeans are starting to feel about the way the United States derives political and diplomatic advantage from its formidable military power contributes to this trend. I hope that our American allies will do what they must so that this little revolution in transatlantic relations occurs harmoniously. For our part, we'll do our best. I have asked Washington to show confidence and patience.

Moïsi: You haven't made any specific mention of Germany.

Védrine: Because in this area—European defense—Germany has not been an obstacle. It's the British and French who have represented the two sides in this debate, and by changing, were in a position to get things going. No other country could have done it. Once the lid was removed in 1998, Germany followed along, as did Italy and Spain, and then the others.

Moïsi: This leads to the broader question of Europe, and your priorities. Which is more important, deepening, with institutional reform, or enlargement, with the redefinition of borders?

Védrine: I repeat: these things are directly and intimately linked. Let us make a success of the enlargement we need, so that the European project emerges stronger and not destroyed! For ten years, from 1989 to 1999, Europeans were divided on enlargement—not between those who were for and those who were against, but between maximalists and demagogues on one side and those who supported a controlled enlargement on the other. What an outcry there was in Brussels each time European Affairs Minister Pierre Moscovici or I backed this line before the EU fifteen! "What about the moral imperative of enlargement?"

they used to ask us aggressively. And I'm not even talking about the tone used by the press in the candidate countries. This gives you a sense of how confused the thinking was! Nonetheless, we had the duty to say and repeat that we had not done all we had over the decades only to see Europe dissolve in a botched enlargement; we didn't do all of that so the candidates themselves could enter a Europe that didn't work, in a sort of Pyrrhic victory. Ultimately it was the reasonable line, our line, that prevailed. This big enlargement will nevertheless be a disruption, and we're preparing for it.

Moïsi: What's new is that we've put all the candidates on the same starting line. Yet we still foresee a first category of country getting to the finish line in 2005 or 2006, if not sooner.

Védrine: Indeed, we put everyone—the six from 1999 and the six from 2000—on the same starting line. It's like a regatta. But one cannot speak about "categories" anymore; we have decided to treat each country according to its own criteria. Since Helsinki, we no longer think in terms of "groups," "waves," or "categories." Nor are the fifteen setting abstract deadlines anymore. This is a better way.

Moïsi: A case-by-case basis? Isn't this another way to hide our lack of enthusiasm?

Védrine: Not at all! The fifteen realized that thinking in terms of categories or groups of countries was in contradiction with the idea that the negotiations would be serious, adapted to each country, and destined to resolve each problem. We also rejected the idea of arbitrarily setting entry dates in advance for each candidate. What we did do was agree to set a date by which the union needed to have its own house in order before it would be ready to welcome the candidates that had finished their preparations—2003. With the institutional reforms agreed at the December 2000 European Council in Nice, we are well on track.

Moïsi: Shouldn't we have been more ambitious?

Védrine: But we are being ambitious. Michel Barnier, Romano Prodi, and the Belgians had from the start proposed to extend the intergovernmental council's (IGC's) agenda to the elaboration of a "major reform," or even a constitution for Europe, but no one was ready to draw the necessary consequences for enlargement—to accept its eventual deferral. Finally we decided in Helsinki to begin with institutional reform, to pick up where the European Council in Feira, Portugal, left off, and to extend the agenda of the conference, notably, to the question of "enhanced cooperation." This was both a wise and an ambitious decision.

It's worth remembering that the goal is to be ready to welcome new members starting in 2003. But let's be clear: we're going to be living for the next ten to twenty years with a major enlargement process that will disrupt European order. This is what I've been saying since 1997, and it's what led me in 1998 to ask Jacques Attali to write a report on how a "Europe of Thirty" would work. It also led me and German foreign minister Joschka Fischer to launch joint work by our two ministries on the same subject in fall 1998.

Moïsi: Are we moving toward a Europe made up, as we used to say, of concentric circles—with a hard core surrounded by looser and wider circles? Or would it be more accurate to use the image of a first class Europe, followed by a second or even third class Europe?

Védrine: What everyone finally recognizes is that you can't just transpose to this much wider Europe the same mechanisms that have allowed us to function so far. It would completely paralyze decision-making. Look how cumbersome the system is at fifteen!

To avoid paralysis or dilution, we've inevitably got to distinguish between what we'll do at twenty-seven, thirty, or more, and what those countries that decide to move forward together will do. It would be an illusion to believe that we can preserve, let alone create, among thirty members the same types of common policies as those we instituted when we were six and that we now pursue as fifteen. The links among the thirty will exist—for example, the single market—but they will be less tight, and the situations will be more diverse.

Thus we've got to put together a new driving force. How? Several possibilities have been put forward: a hard core always made up of the same group of countries—this is Jacques Delors' idea—or diverse groups on a case-by-case or project-by-project basis, according to the "variable geometry" principle.

Moïsi: All this is hard to explain to the public. What we have is a Europe that is a hybrid and is almost federal (in the area of the single currency), but which still mainly follows intergovernmental principles when it comes to foreign and security policy (though we've made more progress in these areas than many realize, not least by putting greater emphasis on regional structures). This kind of Europe is not an easy puzzle to figure out! How can we get people's hearts behind such a construct?

Védrine: Europe's diversity is a fact. It is a source of complications, but also of richness. It's no use regretting that we didn't emerge from a blank piece of paper. How can we move forward? Let's take a closer look.

A system of concentric circles is indefensible. This would be Dante's Inferno in reverse, with the lucky ones in the center and those on the periphery left to their own fate, without hope. By contrast, the difference between those who are part of the euro system and those who are not *yet* part of it is very different, since the latter have the possibility of joining the former. What about permanently setting up a hard core, as Jacques Delors proposes? It's tempting in theory. But which countries would be ready to join it, and with how much more federalist integration? How could we get it accepted by others?

The growing realization of the consequences of the major enlargement ahead of us is going to prompt this debate over the coming months. We saw Joschka Fischer's federalist proposal as a long-term prospect.

The most ingenious, effective, and realistic suggestion seems to me to be variable geometry: the countries that want to move forward beyond common policies can do so. These are not always the same countries, depending on the subjects at hand. That's why we say *variable* geometry, as compared to a *single* hard core always made up of the same countries. You'll find that this flexible formula will be of interest not only to the "big countries," like France, Britain, Germany, Italy, or later Poland, but also to others, depending on the subjects. A major accomplishment of the Nice summit was to make enhanced cooperation easier, and I believe that this mechanism can help us to make really significant progress in the future.

In any case, this differentiation will come about. Either by negotiation or de facto, especially if the refusal of some countries to reform the enhanced cooperation mechanism means that it remains the one foreseen in the treaty, as inflexible as it is impractical. If that is the case, we'll pursue our goals in separate groups of interested countries, as we did for Ariane, Airbus, Eurêka, the euro, or European defense.

Moïsi: There are countries that obviously belong to Europe, but not necessarily to the European Union: Russia today, maybe Turkey, even if its candidacy has now been formally accepted. Wouldn't we be better off, one way or another—but more clearly—making this type of distinction?

Védrine: This brings us back to the question of borders. The question is to know where and when we will draw the dividing line.

In the future, besides the question of its relationship with the United States, one of the big questions for the EU's common foreign policy will be to define its relationship with its big neighbors to the east, southeast, and south: Russia, the Middle East, and Maghreb. And to define where the limit between potential members and partners lies. Beyond those countries with a vocation to become EU members, there are in fact several large neighboring countries with which the union must establish a "strategic partnership." This expression is a bit tarnished now, but it accurately reflects what is needed.

Moïsi: Is it accurate to say that Europe is still an "influence multiplier" for France? Is there something about the European formula that is outmoded, or even self-destructive, as many "sovereignists" think?

Védrine: Self-destructive? Not at all! Europe is not a black hole. The risk, if there is one, would be more likely to come from uncontrolled globalization, whereas Europe is a regulating factor. But I would not say—or no longer say—that Europe is automatically an influence multiplier for us. That was true until the beginning of the 1990s, when it was made up of fewer countries and had a different commission and parliament. Today we're dealing with a more complex and more unstable system, where the point of equilibrium between the national influences and the institutions is harder to define in advance, where relationships are less harmonious, roles less well defined, results less predictable, and less often close to our line. And this will become more and more often the case. From now on, each time we make an institutional decision, in particular, when we put new mechanisms in place—related to the Common Foreign and Security Policy (CFSP) or other matters—we won't be able to do so without asking ourselves how it will work in ten years, in a Europe widened to include more than twenty or twenty-five countries. We want the strongest possible Europe in the future. And we want to continue to see the strongest possible French influence, whatever structures we end up with.

Thus the importance of the debate that is developing today. Two types of solutions have been proposed: pragmatic ones, which seek to give room for maneuver in this future enlarged Europe to states that want to do more together; and federalist ones, which call for a two-speed Europe, with the center consisting of a hard core of a few countries (a "federation of nation-states" or "center of gravity"). Choosing one path or the other will be a historic choice and it must be done democratically. For the moment it's through "enhanced cooperation" that we'll be able to give the EU the means to move forward and the framework to implement its most ambitious projects, if they're agreed to. And this is the way to do so without provoking a theoretical dispute about the nature of the union.

MOÏSI: There was much criticism of the Nice European Council under the French presidency. What's your own view?

VÉDRINE: The results achieved under the whole French presidency (July–December 2000), and not just Nice, are very important. Many concrete problems were resolved, for example, the European company statute, which had been blocked for thirty-two years, and the agreement on savings taxes, which had been blocked for the past three years. The structures of European defense were created and the procedures defined. Progress was made on the fight against international crime, food security, maritime security, the mobility of teachers and students and harmonization in the area of transportation. An action program for social progress was agreed on. The charter on fundamental rights was adopted. We also improved the functioning of the European General Affairs Council, to restore its coordinative role. And we made some diplomatic breakthroughs, like the accession partnership agreement with Turkey and the management of the change of regime in Yugoslavia.

Moïsi: Yes, but it was in the area of institutional reform that people put their faith in France.

Védrine: I am well aware of the expectations placed on France, but I wanted to underline that, under any other presidency, this set of results would be praised.

As for institutions, let me take a step back. At Maastricht, the EU twelve (at the time) decided to call for a new IGC on institutional improvements, to be convened after the treaty was ratified. This conference took place in Amsterdam in 1996–97 and resulted in failure (without anyone speaking of a Dutch failure, and rightly so). During this period, pressure from the central and east European countries to join the union grew constantly, and more and more member-states began to see a big enlargement as the union's top priority.

Moïsi: This wasn't the case for France?

Védrine: France believed that the accession of the new democracies would be a positive historic step, but that to proceed with a massive new enlargement without first improving the decisionmaking procedures in the EU would have been irresponsible, for the candidate countries as well as for the union, because this could result in dilution or paralysis. In the summer of 1997, however, only three countries thought this way: France, Italy, and Belgium. Ultimately, in 1999, the fifteen came to see this necessity and were only too content to set the date for the conclusion of this IGC to fall under the French presidency, since they were well aware of how difficult it would be! We accepted this in a European spirit. This IGC was thus opened under the Portuguese presidency and we then took over the presidency in July 2000.

Moïsi: What were the subjects on the agenda, and the objectives?

Védrine: We had four main objectives, basically, the "leftovers" from Amsterdam that the fifteen had stumbled over. First, to extend qualified majority voting for community business. This was already the case for 80 percent of EU decisions before Nice, and it will now be the case for 90 percent. Nearly all the governments had difficulty going beyond that.

Second, to limit the number of commissioners. On this issue, given the resistance of countries that wanted to keep "their" commissioner, the best we could do was reach agreement on the principle of a ceiling. Yet this itself is very important because the principle will be established in the treaty; the union will have to work out the details before its membership reaches twenty-seven.

Third, to make enhanced cooperation easier, so that a small group of countries can do more. Doing this was impractical under the rigid rules established at Amsterdam. We pretty much accomplished this objective in Nice—now the agreement of eight countries will be enough to launch an enhanced cooperation.

Finally, to give the four "big" countries, the most populous ones, a less undervalued weight in the enlarged union. And it was on this point that, as expected, we had the most difficult discussions. These ended with less reweighting than we might have hoped for, but it was none the less a significant reform.

Moïsi: Then why all the criticism?

Védrine: In fact, a number of countries are very satisfied with the results, given their desires or their apprehensions. Also, many of the criticisms came from institutions—like the European Parliament or the European Commission—or from those who still hope for the sudden establishment of the United States of Europe, and who thus find the progress made at Nice negligible. These critics invoke democracy and the will of people but act as if the European presidency should be an all-powerful tyrant for six months! The EU presidency must scrupulously respect the decisions of the democratically elected member states. After having deployed all its resources to persuade member states to give priority to general European interests over their national interests, the presidency cannot ignore their democratically elected leaders when they say that they cannot go any further.

Moïsi: But did France defend positions that were European enough for its appeals to be credible?

Védrine: France's proposal for a ceiling on the number of commissioners was widely understood to be in the interest of the union. The same goes for enhanced cooperation. The insistence on the reweighting of votes was shared by the other "big" and "middle-size" countries. And on qualified majority voting, France moved on the only issue essential for itself—the negotiations over trade in services—whereas other important countries stuck to their vetoes on much more important subjects, like social, fiscal, or immigration policy. Finally, we were very open to German demands regarding what should come after Nice.

Moïsi: Then why so much criticism?

Védrine: The disappointment of the orphans of the project of immediate and fully achieved European integration, and certain commentators' own agendas.

Moïsi: For example, when they talk about French arrogance?

Védrine: A typical stereotype. If the presidency had been held by another nation at this difficult stage that occurs in any important negotiation, then other national stereotypes would have emerged, equally unjustly.

Moïsi: So you'd say it was the least bad possible result, given the circumstances?

Védrine: It was the best possible, given the political and democratic realities in Europe today. No presidency would have accomplished anything better or anything very different. And the result was foreseeable. Failure was not impossible; remember Amsterdam. It would have had serious consequences.

Moïsi: Couldn't a grand French or Franco-German design have overcome these constraints?

Védrine: All who spoke about Europe's future during spring 2000 concluded their speeches with, "But most of all, Nice must be a success." But maybe you think that he who cannot do the least can do the most? To have put on the IGC's agenda the question of an EU constitution, a hard core, or the precise power-sharing arrangements between the union and its member states would in no way have made the IGC easier. On the contrary, that would have exacerbated the divergences and made the Nice agreement impossible. We'll only see more of these difficulties in the post-Nice period. Joschka Fischer, for example, notwithstanding his famous speech about all this, did not ask to put these issues on the agenda. No, first, and most important, we had to overcome the Amsterdam stalemate. If Nice had been a second failure, after Amsterdam, there would have been serious speculation about the future of Europe. Instead, we have a solid base to stand on as we consider the future.

Moïsi: Did cohabitation hurt the French presidency?

Védrine: I do not believe so.

Moïsi: Some commentators believe that the Nice summit marks the end of a certain Europe, dominated by France?

Védrine: Some are indeed out of touch with what the union had already become many years ago. The Nice negotiations revealed nothing that we didn't know already: we are no longer in the era of the Europe of Six and the Treaty of Rome. Since then there has been the single market, Maastricht, and Amsterdam; there are now fifteen member states; the commission has twenty members and will have more. The European Parliament has 626 members, and at Nice this number was raised to 732, for a union of twenty-seven countries. We opened accession negotiations with twelve candidates, and there are almost ten other potential candidates in Europe. France won't be holding the rotating presidency again until 2008. The construction of Europe has long been based on compromise between the differing conceptions of France, Germany, and others. But I am convinced that France will maintain its capacity to put forth ideas, influence others, and bring them along if it remains imaginative and determined.

Moïsi: Franco-German relations did not seem harmonious in Nice, which is a nice way of putting it. Have we begun a different phase—more distant or more quarrelsome—in our relations?

Védrine: Franco-German relations evolve with reality. After the irreversible achievements of the de Gaulle-Adenauer, Giscard-Schmidt, and Mitterrand-Kohl periods, we have entered a new period in which the unified Germany wants to be a "normal" country that defends its interest without any sort of complex. In the name of what could we possibly challenge Germany's right to do so? Why get worked up about it? Personally, I never have. Chancellor Schroeder is the incarnation of this new Germany. We need to base our thinking on this new reality.

Moïsi: But did France and Germany act together in the framework of the IGC?

Védrine: For much of it, yes, on other issues, no. For France to accept the German reality does not mean to automatically accept all of Germany's requests. Just as for Germany, recognizing the French reality has never meant, even before unification, automatically swallowing all French ideas. In the framework of the IGC, France and Germany basically defended the same positions on the commission, enhanced cooperation, and the post-Nice agenda. On qualified majority voting they were flexible, but both had a red line: France on cultural policy, Germany on asylum, free movement, and immigration.

Moïsi: Yes, but there was big disagreement on the reweighting of votes.

Védrine: Like us, Germany wanted the weight of "big" countries to be better recognized, and this main objective was achieved. Within this group of big countries, Germany also wanted its own weight to be augmented even more. We managed to satisfy this demand with a demographic safety net, which will take population into account in EU votes, and reinforced Germany's representation in the European Parliament. But we preserved the spirit of the system: the founding parity among France, Germany, Italy (and later Great Britain) within the European Council. This is not a bad result. The negotiations on the reweighting of votes pitted a number of countries against each other, but the main thing is that we managed to reach agreement.

Moïsi: Yes, but is it still possible to talk about a Franco-German motor?

Védrine: I'm glad you used the word "motor," which I've always preferred to "couple," which is too introverted. Motor better expresses the desirable leadership potential of these two countries vis-à-vis the rest of Europe. This is, in any case, how things went for thirty-five years, until the ratification of the Maastricht Treaty. Afterwards, at the end of the Kohl era, this relationship found itself somewhat altered by German reunification and the reticence of the *Länder* to go further toward European construction. Then, in a way, it was overcome by its own success with the creation of the euro, and then disrupted by the changes in personnel, both in Paris and in Bonn/Berlin.

The final Kohl years (1997–98) and Gerhard Schroeder's first year—when he had both to put in place a new government and to hold the EU presidency (during the difficult financial negotiations of Agenda 2000, which were concluded in Berlin in March 1999)—were more or less lost. Starting in summer 1999, it became possible to get the Franco-German relationship started up again. The way to do this was not through gadgets like "joint embassies," but by working together to develop a long-term vision for Europe—how far could it go geographically and institutionally? This is the big job that I began with Joschka Fischer in fall 1998 and that was already producing fruits in Helsinki, since that's in part how we managed to get around some of the differences we had over the past few years on enlargement. Some of this thinking, by the way, inspired his federalist speech in Berlin. This work is still going on at the level of the president, prime minister, and chancellor.

To make enlargement possible, we had to have a new debate about the role of each country in the union's institutions. This was inevitably going to be difficult, and it is now behind us. It does not mean that we have lost the capacity to work together on new projects. Look at the Benelux: it's not going to disappear just because Belgium and the Netherlands ran up against each other during the discussion of reweighting! Now that we have the Nice agreement, let's look to the future.

Moïsi: Still, the impression of a certain emotional and sentimental void—a new sort of gap—exists between our two countries. Mssrs. Schroeder and Fischer have even admitted as much.

Védrine: It's a good sign that the chancellor and the foreign minister are worried about it; that should help us move forward. We've noticed that when the Franco-German motor is weakened, nothing comes to replace it. At the heart of any formula for getting Europe going again, hard core or variable geometry, you've got France and Germany. But we also know that this duo must today be joined by others.

Moïsi: But if the Franco-German motor is no longer what it used to be, and if nothing new has come along to replace it, do we not see on the horizon a sort of "Club of Three," within which Britain would play the full role that it has every right to play alongside France and Germany?

Védrine: Don't be so quick to draw conclusions about the Franco-German relationship. What you say about Great Britain is true in the defense area, on the basis of new Franco-British agreement since 1998. The power of these two partnerships to draw others along, if they were more united, would be strong. But it seems difficult to go further while Britain has not joined the euro. And its hesitation over institutions doesn't help either.

Moïsi: It's not that simple. First of all, not all the other European countries are at the same level of engagement and they have very different means of acting and influencing.

Védrine: Thus the different methods of cooperation. Still, there is a growing basis of common references, which, by the way, justified the strength of the reactions to the risk of seeing Austria violate these values. Today, each of the fifteen EU members participates as an equal in the common policies. If you think about how it will be with enhanced cooperation, you can easily see that everyone, at some point, will have a key role to play in one area or another of the future common foreign and security policy, and each will be a "motor" in some specific area. There are plenty of examples of this.

Moïsi: Some have said Nice consecrated de facto German leadership. Do you agree?

Védrine: I do not think Germany wants to or can govern Europe! Thus I continue to believe that a Franco-German understanding is essential, even if it is insufficient, because all member states matter. I also think that, as Joschka Fischer so rightly says, Franco-German tensions are "productive." Well, let's produce!

Moïsi: After Nice, are the doors of the union henceforth open to candidates for accession?

VÉDRINE: Yes, at Helsinki the fifteen made the commitment to be ready to welcome as new members, staring at the end of 2002 or early 2003, the candidate countries that would then be ready to enter, that is to say, to live up to the *acquis communautaire*. Given the time it takes for ratification, this meant we needed an agreement by December 2000 in Nice. Thus we kept to our word. This is also part of the success of Nice.

MOÏSI: France is accused of dragging its feet in the enlargement negotiations.

VÉDRINE: I am aware of these suspicions about our motives. They are unfounded and unjust. France has from the beginning said very clearly that the accession negotiations must be very serious for enlargement to succeed, in the interest of members as well as candidates—who want to join the union because it works. What good would it do them to join a paralyzed union without common policies? Apparently this is still too soon for some, since that was enough to set off a sort of prosecution and periodic intimidation campaigns.

MOÏSI: What do you mean by that?

VÉDRINE: These criticisms of so-called French obstruction have been coming from several sources: certain member states that, faithful to their purely free trade conception of Europe, have always given priority to widening over deepening; several others that were using enlargement to particular countries as part of a regional strategy of patronage or sponsorship to reinforce their influence in the enlarged Europe of tomorrow; certain candidate states that, having trouble making the necessary domestic reforms (which are in fact difficult), wanted to find a shortcut around the main difficulties of the negotiation by getting the union to set a date for their accession immediately and arbitrarily; and finally, generous pro-European circles, who see enlargement as a moral duty and who are discovering only now(!), painfully, how much previous enlargements have already reduced the capacity of the union of fifteen to deepen.

MOÏSI: So you deny any French obstructionism?

VÉDRINE: Look at the progress made under the French presidency! The negotiations are led under the aegis of the rotating presidency, but in practice by the European Commission, under the authority of Commissioner Verheugen. Over the course of the second half of 2000, the union presented the twelve candidates with nearly one hundred negotiating positions, which enabled discussions to begin on more than forty chapters of the *acquis communautaire* and, as of early 2001, to conclude on thirty of them. Moreover, the union started to address some of the most serious issues, by examining the requests for transition periods presented by the candidates. The union's positive response to some of these requests made it possible to provisionally close some important chapters of the *acquis* with certain candidates, like free trade in services, free circulation of goods, or social policy. But today 500 requests for "transition periods" have been put forward by the candidates, and others are sure to come. If we were to accept all of them, there would be no more common policies or a single market. If they are all refused, there would be no enlargement. Thus we are going to negotiate, candidate by candidate, until we reach an agreement on the whole acceptable for the union.

Moïsi: Are you still differentiating among candidates?

VÉDRINE: We continually reaffirm this principle. We'll take the state of preparation of each candidate country into account.

Moïsi: When?

VÉDRINE: As soon as they're ready, starting in 2003. From that time, it will only be a matter of when they are able to meet and apply the *acquis communautaire*.

Moïsi: Is there still ambiguity regarding Turkey?

VÉDRINE: No ambiguity, but a different situation. As I already mentioned, Turkey's European character was—and remains—debated. Many European leaders think that a strategic partnership would be better adapted to the situation than accession. But given that promises were made to Turkey years ago, and since the most modern forces in Turkey depend on these commitments, the fifteen finally decided in 1999 to accept—to take note of, if you will—Turkey's candidacy. But accession negotiations were not opened, since Turkey was really too far from meeting the Copenhagen criteria.[1] In the meantime, under the French presidency, we concluded an Accession Partnership with Turkey, to help it come closer to meeting these goals.

MOÏSI: What about the Balkan countries?

VÉDRINE: The union is working on "association and stabilization agreements" with the Balkan countries that are not yet candidates. These are key elements in our Balkan policy, which is really going to be able to develop thanks to the change in Belgrade. The eventual accession of these countries is something to look forward to, but it is not a current issue.

MOÏSI: Despite all this, should we not regret the stalling of the European project?

VÉDRINE: It depends whether you judge it compared to where we started or according to utopia or idealism. Compared to prewar Europe, or even to the 1950s, the progress we have made is staggering—a true metamorphosis, unprecedented in the history of the world. But if you measure the Rome, Maastricht, Amsterdam, and Nice treaties against the idea of the United States of Europe, if you live in the expectation of the abolition of national governments and parliaments and compare what we've achieved with total political integration, then the result is indeed frustrating. But this is the reality of Europe. This is the *democratic* reality of the Europe of Fifteen and it will be even more so for the Europe of Thirty. This may be regrettable, but in that case we should have created a true integrated and federal Europe at the time of the Europe of Six, when it may have been possible.

MOÏSI: Still, at Nice you adopted measures for the "post-Nice" agenda. This proves that you—the fifteen—were not entirely satisfied with Nice.

1. At its 1993 summit in Copenhagen, the EU set out the criteria that new members would have to meet. These included stability of institutions (including democracy, the rule of law, human rights, and protection of minorities); a functioning market economy; adherence to the aims of political, economic, and monetary union; and adaptation of administrative structures.

VÉDRINE: No, on the contrary, it shows that, having resolved at Nice the problems that were not resolved at Amsterdam, the fifteen were able to start thinking about the future and a new stage, which would not have been possible had Nice been a failure. Chancellor Schroeder needed us to commit to the future clarification of the division of labor among the union, member states, and regions, without which the *Länder* and the Bundesrat would have threatened not to ratify Nice. We took this into account and agreed that a new IGC, in 2004, would address this issue of relative competencies. It will also look to simplify the treaties, clarify the status of the charter on fundamental rights, and examine the role of national parliaments in the European construction process. This IGC, which must be preceded by a big democratic debate, need not be a long one. But you can be sure that a lot of the ideas recently put forward will be part of this debate: on a constitution, a "hard core" (I use this phrase in a general sense because it was the first to be used, starting in 1994, but there are a lot of different formulations and concepts), a federation of nation states, enhanced political integration, etc. Of course, all these terms have many meanings and will need to be clarified: the constitution, or a federation of nation states, could just as well describe the current distribution of powers between the union and the member states as it could a massive transfer of competencies and sovereignty to the "federal" level; you could have a federalism of integration. And it is also possible in a "federal" framework to redistribute competencies in the name of "subsidiarity," the idea that decisionmaking should take place at the closest level possible to the citizens. This is a great debate in which everyone in Europe will have to take a position.

MOÏSI: In particular, on the question of the hard core?

VÉDRINE: Yes, the partisans of much greater political integration, increasingly concerned about the consequences of enlargement, will insist more and more on putting the idea of a hard core, or *avant-garde*, at the top of the agenda. But this will be fought, both within the current union and among the candidates, by the adversaries of a two-speed Europe. If some member states wanted to move toward a hard core and could agree on who would be in it, there would be two options: leave the Eurogroup, which is the new name for the Euro zone—the countries participating in the single currency; or develop several enhanced cooperations among selected countries, as permitted by the Nice Treaty, and then observe that they happen to involve the same countries, forming a de facto hard core—which will be less difficult for those who are not (yet) part of it to accept.

Moïsi: What are your immediate priorities?

Védrine: To clearly redefine the Franco-German entente; to ratify the Nice Treaty without delay; take advantage of all it offers, including the expansion of majority voting and enhanced cooperation; to further harmonize economic policies in the Euro zone; to negotiate accessions well, to make a success of enlargement; and to launch and animate among the fifteen and among the candidates the great democratic dialogue that will get us ready for 2004 and clarify how power will be divided between the EU and its member states. Will the EU ultimately be a federation of nation states, or a new type of confederation? Something else? How are power, sovereignty, and competencies distributed? How and by whom are sovereignty, or European responsibilities, exercised? Will this be something for all twenty-seven or will there be an open and widely accepted *avant-garde*? At this point, none of these options can be excluded. Let us not preempt the debate that the French government will enrich with its proposals, but which must allow all to express themselves and democracy to decide. Europe has been building itself in an original way for more than fifty years now, becoming an institutional category of its own and contradicting the naysayers. It will continue to do so.

Common Foreign Policy, National Foreign Policies

DOMINIQUE MOÏSI: In the era of the Common Foreign and Security Policy (CFSP), doesn't being the foreign minister of a European Union (EU) country—to use a deliberately provocative expression—mean representing a species in the process of rapid extinction? Doesn't it mean preparing to shut down a business that had been an exclusively national one?

HUBERT VÉDRINE: To a provocative question, let me give you a straight answer: no!

MOÏSI: This is a surprising answer, to say the least.

VÉDRINE: France's foreign policy will continue in one form or another.

MOÏSI: But how can we define and justify the maintenance of national policies at a time when Europe aspires to endow itself with a "common foreign and security policy": are national policies the necessary bases, or pillars, or are they an obstacle and an anachronism?

VÉDRINE: National policies are the bases and pillars on which to build. What would be the basis of a common foreign and security policy if you were to close up the "national shops" it lives off? Remember the debate about the European currency: should it be *single* or *common?* We decided in favor of a single currency because national sovereignty in currency matters was becoming a fiction, especially for non-Germans, since we were in any case moving toward a [deutsche] mark zone. Despite this, Chancellor Kohl had the strategic intelligence to understand that even a mark zone would, in reality, be subordinate to the dollar. The finance ministers and the central bank governors all realized that this sovereignty was becoming purely theoretical.

The situation is not at all the same when it comes to the area of foreign and security policy. First, currency is one thing and foreign policy is something else, something that has its roots in each country's own particular mentality and that you cannot change by decree. France has had a real foreign policy for a long time. With more or less intensity, depending on the region or issue, this foreign policy covers the whole world, deals with every subject, and also covers economic and cultural affairs. It is a global policy, both geographically and thematically. No French politician is ready to abandon it. This possibility has never been submitted to any vote, by any government. No treaty, neither Maastricht nor Amsterdam, envisaged it. You can say the same about Great Britain, of some other countries, and more and more about Germany. For all these reasons, what we decided to implement was a *common* foreign policy, at least to begin with.

MOÏSI: How?

VÉDRINE: By common actions and progressive convergence. We must not get rid of national foreign policies but must take advantage of them for our common foreign policy. And this is the task, together with the ministers of foreign affairs of the member states, of "Mr. CFSP," Javier Solana. Besides, the union's external relations need to work better. Commissioner Chris Patten has taken this on. At the end of the day, the common foreign policy must represent value added. Yes to common strategy. Yes to common actions. No to the least common denominator. No to harmonization from the bottom up.

Moïsi: But is it the specific field of diplomatic activity that makes for the main difference between the single currency and the common foreign policy, or is it just the way France acts in these areas? Is this an objective or a subjective difference? Are the things that we can dress up our foreign policy interest in—sovereignty, the flag, emotions—of an essentially different nature from those of our currency, for example?

Védrine: Yes, because this concerns our history, because it concerns our underlying mentality, the most personal views of our citizens, and because it cannot be changed by decree. You can't just decide that on a given date, French, British, or other views about relations with the United States or Africa will no longer be valid and will be replaced by a common view fixed in Brussels! Especially in a Europe of twenty or thirty! That won't work. We've got to take a whole range of things into account: national mentalities, history, zones of influence, established relations, the languages people speak, their habits, where they send their children to be educated, signed agreements, the obligations that derive from them, military links, etc. That's why, I repeat, we wisely decided—and have started—to build a common, and not single, foreign policy. Which is, itself, a big ambition. After that, we'll see. This policy can only be strong if our European institutions work well; if we manage to make the most of the Mr. CFSP job—Javier Solana was best placed to do that—and if we encourage in this spirit good cooperation between him and Chris Patten. But also if this effort is constantly irrigated, fed, and stimulated by strong and well-coordinated national policies. What would we have to gain today by dissolving ourselves into a European average? And especially, what would Europe gain from this? Most member states share this point of view.

Moïsi: Let me back up for a moment. German identity is intimately linked to the currency. For the Germans, renouncing their currency, joining the euro and abandoning the mark, meant renouncing an important part of their identity. For the French, on the other hand, their international identity seems, if I can put it this way, to represent one of the essential components of their national identity.

Védrine: This is clear, but I repeat, you can't conclude from it that these two areas can be run in the same way. The two differ in both nature and malleability. I don't rule out that one day, a long time from now, once mentalities have converged, we can think about moving from a common to a single policy. For now, we have to move forward.

MOïSI: How can we reconcile two necessities: (1) for Europe to manage in foreign policy to do what it already does in commercial policy, which is to say, to speak with a single voice, and therefore be much more credible compared to the other major countries, particularly the United States; and (2) to avoid harmonization from below, with the lowest common denominator as the only possible basis for agreement?

VÉDRINE: How to reconcile them? By working to get a dynamic consensus at the highest possible level. In foreign policy, the lowest common denominator consists of peace, human rights, and development. This is important, but it's not enough to constitute a policy in the operational sense of the term. We would be irresponsible if we were to allow French foreign policy to dissolve into a well-intentioned but stereotypical message of humanism, backed up by a few aid programs calculated in euros. The British, in particular, think like we do on this subject, and so do many other member states. For the sake of our own countries and their histories, as well as for the sake of the progress that we anticipate for Europe, it is our duty to continue to pursue active and inventive foreign policies. Of course, it is also our duty to avoid allowing them to contradict one another and even to bring them closer and closer together. Nearly every day we face the choice between, on the one hand, accepting a compromise and renouncing something important for us, in order to encourage a common European position, and on the other, refusing a consensus too far from where we stand, which would oblige us to give up too much, to better preserve the later development of a stronger European policy. This is how the day-to-day construction of the CFSP works.

MOïSI: In this context, the role of Mr. CFSP is particularly delicate, because he's not only got to assert his identity vis-à-vis the president of the commission, Mr. Prodi, vis-à-vis the commissioner for external affairs, Mr. Patten, not to mention the commissioner for enlargement, Mr. Verheugen, but he's also got to try to bring the different national positions closer together. He's got to facilitate compromises, even while his own areas of responsibility are badly defined.

VÉDRINE: Indeed, this new job is delicate. That's the very reason why, in 1999, we chose a man for that job who is subtle, politically gifted, and very experienced internationally, given his former positions as secretary general of the North Atlantic Treaty Organization (NATO) and foreign minister of Spain. He's got to make the common part of the union's foreign policy stronger, more coherent, and more visible. There's plenty to do! We're helping him. You're right: he's also got to figure out where he fits in vis-à-vis the president of the commission and the other commissioners. He's in the process of doing so. With the foreign affairs ministers of the member states, he's got to participate actively in the elaboration of the widest possible consensus. And he can only do that if all the others try, in good faith, to deepen and extend the part of European foreign policy that's already made in common. He's got to explain, to articulate, and to concentrate on certain key issues.

MOÏSI: There are some areas that fall more naturally under the common foreign policy, and others that will remain specifically national. In the case of France, what will remain French in foreign policy terms?

VÉDRINE: It's hard to distinguish between the national and the European. As far as the eye can see, I am convinced that there will be a global French foreign policy, and also British, German, and other ones. But in more and more areas it will be increasingly combined with a European policy consisting of commercial agreements, financial arrangements, aid, and common positions and strategies. Whether we're talking about the summits that the EU holds with the United States, Russia, Japan, China, or India; the negotiations with candidate countries; the meetings with associated countries, with Africa, and with Latin America; there is already in all these areas a European Union policy that corresponds to the *C* in the acronym CFSP. This policy results from the discussions we had among the fifteen well in advance. It's an extension of ourselves, of our views, of our propositions, even though it may have passed through the filter of compromise, which goes without saying. But it's one of the ways in which we express ourselves.

If you consider all the big subjects, foreign policies as strong and complete as those of, say, France and Great Britain, could only hypothetically be *replaced* one day by a *single* European policy if this European policy proved itself capable of handling all the diplomatic, political, economic, strategic, and cultural aspects that such a policy implies, for example, regarding relations with the United States or Russia. This policy would also have to prove itself capable of acquiring the same capacity to react and the same maneuverability as national policies. I don't know when we'll get to that point; this is a relatively new ambition. But if it was never reached at six or nine, or ten, twelve, or fifteen, how could it be reached at twenty-seven? I put my faith, instead, in using smart and pragmatic methods to build something original, case by case.

Moïsi: But nevertheless, is it not possible to distinguish between areas that lend themselves particularly well to national action and others where, on the contrary, European action makes sense?

Védrine: It's difficult to divide things up like that in a rigid way. Following this logic would lead you to say that Africa, for example, should be a national policy because it's a traditional zone of influence for France. But at the same time, European aid policy, through the Lomé Convention, is very important for Africa, at least so long as France manages to save these agreements, which are threatened every time they're renegotiated. Thus you could also say that Africa should be a community policy. And that would be very restrictive. However, the French authorities—in particular, Charles Josselin, the minister in charge of cooperation and Francophonie—also play a key role in the elaboration and implementation of the Lomé policy, and aid and development policy in general. Thus these things have to be dealt with together.

Let's take another example. France has a particular way of looking at relations with the United States. We've talked about this. It can't be said that the instinctive approach of most of our European partners is identical to our own. But this is a fundamental matter for France, because the question of relations with the United States is at the heart of international relations today. It will be a long time before you'll see all the other Europeans sharing our vision on this matter, except in the area of trade. Should we therefore give it up? No. France cannot force others to adopt all of its positions, but the others cannot ask France to renounce them either. We've got to seek convergence, but it will take time.

Moïsi: Are you saying that the more French foreign policy remains French and preserves the specificity of its vision, of its understanding of international affairs, the more it contributes to Europe by adding to its diversity?

Védrine: Don't pretend to be surprised by this apparent paradox. But yes, France has to hold onto a potential all its own. It's got to preserve a useful and productive difference, thus a capacity for initiative. This is a plus, added value for the whole of Europe. Now, of course, there are different ways of doing this. And again, it's also true for other European countries.

Moïsi: In your view, we enrich Europe by the historical depth of our views and by adding to its diversity. But on the other hand, isn't it by sacrificing part of our difference on the altar of Europe that we'll best move the union forward?

Védrine: But we've made these creative compromises a thousand times, we do it every day! But let me repeat: it is necessary that what you end up with be greater than the mere addition of what each party renounces. Let's not have zero-sum games or think about it in terms of losses! I could say the same for each of our European partners, who all contribute something. I would not wish to see them renounce their own particularities for the sole purpose of melting into a European average, the shade of gray you get when you mix up all the colors of the palette. In reality, we would all lose from this.

Moïsi: Thus Europe's strength, including in foreign policy, is its diversity?

Védrine: I really think so. So long as we orchestrate this diversity.

Moïsi: So, France and Britain contribute through their classical vision of great powers and by their traditional conception of power; and Germany contributes through the vision—more modern because more modest—of a country that has been profoundly battered by history?

Védrine: Britain and France have experience with power and a modern world view that takes this into account while going beyond it. As for Germany, it is again planning to carry out its responsibilities on a broader stage. The distinctions are fading.

Moïsi: As for all the others . . .

Védrine: . . . each makes its own contribution. As a result of history, each European country has a particular understanding of a certain region of the world, of a certain type of problem, even beyond the regionalist policies already mentioned. If you add them up they constitute a powerful whole. Greece has a vision of the Balkans, Portugal and Spain of the Mediterranean, the Nordic countries of the northern part of the planet. Indeed, there are European nationals in just about every region of the world. On each subject, you find that there is at least one European country in a position to talk with particular expertise and authority. The political-diplomatic leader on any given subject can easily be a country other than those normally referred to as big countries.

Moïsi: Portugal surely knows East Timor better than does France.

Védrine: That's an example, and the Dutch experience with Indonesia was also useful. We've got to cultivate this richness and variety, not standardize it. Do you realize the accumulated wealth this represents?! We've got to graft onto it a common way of expressing ourselves, a growing coherence, and a way of reducing antagonisms. But don't expect mechanistic transfers to this or that community institution in this area. France will continue to have something to say about all the world's problems.

Moïsi: It's clear that when it comes to analysis, diversity is valuable; that each party contributes through its history, its geography, its differences with common European positions. But when you go from analysis to action, doesn't this diversity become a problem and an obstacle?

Védrine: That's where good institutions can transform diversity into energy. For example, we never could have had the first big Europe–Latin American summit, in Rio in 1999, if it hadn't started out as a French-Spanish initiative, or without the long-standing practice of holding Iberian–Latin American summits. The other Europeans accepted this de facto leadership because it was a plus for all the participants. It's progress for everyone. Take another example: it is clear that the EU position on the Middle East would not be the same if France hadn't led the way, leading the thinking and the evolution of others, for the past twenty years. France's positions are not exactly the same as the current common positions. It maintains its own tone. Yet the European position is much firmer than it would have been without France. There are plenty of other examples. Each time, you've got to look at each particular point to see what you win and what you lose.

Moïsi: Some in Europe—and not just in the Anglo-Saxon world—say that in the name of harmonization from above you promote blockage from below, by defending positions that are unacceptable to other European countries. Examples of this might include relations with the United States, European defense, or whatever at any given time seems a specifically national French interest.

Védrine: Other than the denigration of French foreign policy by some in the Anglo-Saxon and other media, which is like background noise and part of the fight for world influence, I have never heard anyone formulate this criticism, certainly not Madeleine Albright, Robin Cook, or Joschka Fischer. Moreover, this critique could apply to any strong foreign policy, like Britain's. And where does that lead us? Personally, I'm not bothered by this critique, because I have tried to go about all my business in a way that, while certainly forceful, is not arrogant, and that demonstrates the constant search for value added rather than posturing. In any case, it is no longer possible just to reflexively trot out the old criticisms of French foreign policy. What is true, I repeat, is that in Europe we each have our own approach. But we've begun to develop a sort of system of chemical transformation—maybe alchemy would be a better analogy!—such that the richness that results from our diversity reinforces Europe rather than shackles it.

Moïsi: If you take the geographical areas where the French past and French understanding contribute to Europe, you would obviously choose the African continent and the Middle East. What would you say is unique about the French contribution to European policy in these two regions of the world today, starting with Africa?

Védrine: In Africa, a renewed and modernized engagement. In the Middle East, the search for a just solution. But each case is very different.

In Africa, French diplomatic action is targeted at promoting the development of the continent and combating the disinterest of the Americans and the other European partners. Too few European countries are interested in Africa: Belgium, Great Britain, Portugal, Spain a bit, as well, of course, in a different way, as the European Commission. We work with them. In practice, this means maintaining a sufficient flow of public development aid, even if the proportion between aid and trade varies, as is to be expected. This aid needs to be better monitored and better used, but it has to be maintained, and France watches this carefully within multilateral, financial, and other institutions. The president of the republic and the prime minister pay close attention to this. Then there are the conflicts in Africa—twenty of them! We exhort our partners not to let down their guard in the face of such a situation.

On my first trip around Africa, I summed up this policy by the phrase "loyalty, openness, adaptation": demanding loyalty toward our traditional Francophone partners—without interference in their internal affairs, as we demonstrated in Côte d'Ivoire; openness toward Anglophone and Lusophone Africa, as Africa itself is in the process of globalizing; openness toward other partners: French-British initiatives, coordination with Japan on aid, cooperation with Egypt on East Africa, France–South Africa dialogue on southern Africa; French-American and, as much as possible, Euro-American cooperation on peacekeeping in Africa; finally, adaptation, modernization of procedures, methods, and objectives, thanks in particular to Prime Minister Jospin's reform of our cooperation agreements. We remain fraternally engaged alongside Africa, but in different ways.

Moïsi: One more thought about Africa: the old emphasis on intervention, along with the complex networks of financial and political interpenetration between Africa and France, have led to the idea that Africa brings out the best and the worst in the French. The best? A constant interest in the African continent. The worst? The accusation of neocolonialism has been around for a long time. Besides, a certain form of interventionism has returned to us like a boomerang, by bringing back some of the vices of the African system—notably corruption—to certain sectors of French public and economic life.

VÉDRINE: I hope you will allow me to qualify this severe retrospective judgment, even as I would be the first to admit the degree to which things have changed.

You no doubt remember what was called "Cartiérism." Thirty or forty years ago, the editor of *Paris-Match* used to say, "La Corrèze avant le Zambèze!"—a French region in need of development should be taken care of before an African one. On Africa, a certain moralism can led to Cartiérism. It wouldn't be too difficult in Europe today to find a qualified majority, under the pretext of a failure to respect human rights, for example, for cutting off all aid to Africa and saying, "You really aren't very respectable, you don't respect democracy like in Europe. Well then, you're on your own!"

Let's come back to France's record in Africa over the past few decades. If you look back over the great tragedies that have taken place in Africa since most countries got their independence—and there have been a lot of tragedies, accompanied by hundreds of thousands of deaths—if you're honest, you'd have to recognize that *most of Africa's great catastrophes occurred outside France's traditional zone of influence:* Biafra, Ethiopia, Somalia, Uganda, Sudan, Angola, Mozambique, Sierra Leone, Liberia, and others. (The only exceptions are the problems that resulted from the past, like the antagonism between Hutus and Tutsis in Rwanda, Burundi, Uganda, and Zaire, which is still unresolved.) Why don't you thus compare the record of our Africa policy with the record of the policies of other Western countries? Because you can't, because they haven't had an Africa policy. And thus they haven't been criticized. By means that admittedly are no longer appropriate and were sometimes reprehensible, for a long time after independence France brought more security, stability, and development to its African partners than was the case elsewhere, and it brought better protection against great tragedy. But that was another era, another chapter: other forms of cooperation were tolerated then. Today we are in a different phase, Africa is genuinely becoming more independent, and none of these old criticisms could be applied to the African policies of the Jospin government since June 1997. This has become clear by the way we have managed crises in Congo, in Niger, in the Comoros islands, in Côte d'Ivoire since December 1999, among others, without interference, by condemning the use of force and acting constantly to restore constitutional order.

Moïsi: When you compare moralists to Cartiérists, it would be easier to agree if French aid had gone to countries rather than to regimes. The main problem of the African continent is that to aid countries, you've got to work with regimes, and these regimes sometimes divert this aid for their own use. In fact, you end up not aiding African populations, but rather helping the regimes to stay in power, to satisfy much less legitimate and noble ambitions.

Védrine: The comparison that I'm making has to do with things that could go wrong today, not about the past. And your criticism could be applied to all types of aid policy, including international aid; thus the temptation, to avoid being criticized, to say, "Let's not give anyone aid!" Besides, internal funds have been diverted more than international aid. Let me also add that democracy has advanced considerably since François Mitterrand's now famous speech in La Baule in 1990, when he announced that France would link its bilateral cooperation with African countries to their progress in this area. This can be seen in the constitutions that have been put in place, the votes that have been organized, the judgments of international observers, the progress made in justice, media pluralism, etc. Things are moving forward step by step, but in the right direction. The progress is incontestable. The recent changeover of power in Senegal between Abdou Diouf and Abdoulaye Wade and the elections in Ghana in December 2000 are very promising examples for Africa.

Moïsi: One cannot say as much for Côte d'Ivoire over the past year.

Védrine: Indeed, Côte d'Ivoire has been going through a long period of instability. In fact it has been in trouble since the death of former president Felix Houphouët-Boigny in 1993.

Moïsi: France was criticized for its attitude toward the crisis in Côte d'Ivoire.

Védrine: Yes, but with two different types of criticism that were completely contradictory. Some reflexively criticized us for having allegedly played a role in the fall of Konan Bédié or the electoral victory of Laurent Gbagbo, for having been secretly behind, or even against, Alassane Ouattara. Others, on the contrary, denounced us for not interfering and called on us to reestablish democracy. In short, we were criticized for everything and its opposite. Where Africa is concerned, the commentaries and the criticisms are being modernized less quickly than our policies.

Moïsi: What, precisely, is this policy?

Védrine: We have refused to get involved in the internal affairs of Côte d'Ivoire, but we have also refused to turn away; we have said what we have expected of the Ivorians. We clearly condemned the coup d'état that overthrew President Konan Bédié and brought General Gueï to power. We asked the EU to set in motion the procedure we call Article 366 bis, foreseen for this sort of situation, which seeks to reestablish constitutional order through dialogue but under threat of the suspension of cooperation. And we accomplished this. There was a constitutional referendum in June 2000, which all the parties, including Mr. Ouattara, asked their supporters to participate in. And there were presidential elections in October.

Moïsi: Yes, but the supreme court prevented Ouattara from running for office.

Védrine: The supreme court did indeed declare Mr. Ouattara ineligible because he is not Ivorian. We publicly regretted this decision, which affected the meaning of the elections, but they nonetheless took place legally, according to the Ivorian Constitution. Mr. Gbagbo won with 60 percent of the vote and the same level of voter turnout as in the 1995 election of Konan Bédié. No African or Western government contests this any more.

Moïsi: And the problem arose again with the parliamentary elections. You cannot claim that all this was completely democratic.

Védrine: As in the presidential elections, we regretted the invalidation of Ouattara but noted that the legislative elections were held as planned. Our line is now to encourage the Ivorians to overcome the shocks of these events, to consolidate their democracy and reinvigorate their economy, which has sunk. Better cooperation between Côte d'Ivoire and its neighbors is indispensable for that. All our partners share this approach.

Moïsi: If we move to the Middle East, the issues are very different.

Védrine: In fact, it's the opposite situation: France has developed very strong relations there, some derived from history and others built more recently, but it's not in the center of events and hardly has to fight against disengagement! History means Lebanon, Syria, and Egypt. What has been built includes Israel—in a turbulent but real way; and also the Palestinians, the Arabian peninsula, and Jordan. France believes its ideas can contribute to a durable solution to the problem of the Middle East. France has been making these ideas known for nearly twenty years. It played the role of a precursor and over the long term it has exerted a profound influence over the way people think. It did so quite a lot during the final years of the presidency of Valéry Giscard d'Estaing, and even more under François Mitterrand, in particular through his speech to the Knesset in March 1982 and by his subsequent policies. And this approach has since been actively pursued under Jacques Chirac. I'm not a great fan of words standing in for diplomacy, but in this case France has provided an example of actions through words. In the current phase, the priority is on maintaining contacts with each of the parties.

Let's be clear: in reality, American power has dominated the Middle East since Suez, in 1956. Thus it is no recent phenomenon: notwithstanding the premonitions of General de Gaulle, the United States has for forty-five years been the main actor in this region of the world. For a long period it did not try to do very much for peace, absorbed as it was by its unconditional support for Israel and its opposition to the aims of the U.S.S.R. via the radical Arab movements. Now that the negotiations have been started up again under the auspices of the Americans, who are the decisive arbiters, how can France be useful? By having a strong and principled voice, by putting solutions forward, by proposing just formulas, and by maintaining contacts with all the relevant parties. When French ideas, which had been resisted for a long time by the Israelis, the Arabs, and the Americans, started to become the reference point for everyone, the Americans took back the lead for obvious reasons. Our own role, which is in great demand, is that of a facilitator who is in a position to talk with all the protagonists, without standing in for them in their direct dialogue. Our role is to preserve, or even to strengthen, contacts with each of them—this is what we did with the Israelis under Ehud Barak—but also with the Americans, while associating the other Europeans as well. The search for peace would doubtless not have attained its current stage without the steps that France has undertaken for twenty years. If preserved and kept intact, this capacity should inspire European action.

Moïsi: If you look at French policy in the Middle East today, several concerns stand out: a concern for realism, in the sense that we don't want to play the role of the Greek chorus, commenting on events or condemning what happens from the heights of our impotence . . .

Védrine: Rather than flatter ourselves for being the only ones who are right, we prefer to move things forward. The Middle East needs this.

Moïsi: I think that France under Valéry Giscard d'Estaing was right on the level of analysis. But the method it used—open criticism of the Camp David process—condemned France to isolation, notwithstanding this pertinent analysis. In fact, we did more to create transatlantic misunderstanding than we did to advance the cause of peace! What is critical, however, and probably new today, is the realistic idea of complementarity, rather than our trying to substitute ourselves in the key American role. Neither France nor Europe can pretend to represent a real alternative.

Védrine: Sure, but just getting Europeans not to compete with the United States, as the Americans want, is not enough to ensure that American policy is right. If, in fact, it is not desirable for us to compete with the Americans, it's because none of the Israelis, the Syrians, the Lebanese, or the Palestinians are expecting that from us. That's why we've got to be capable of talking to all the parties, including the Americans and the Israelis. It's on this condition that we can be heard and can influence things. We're not playing a separate game.

Moïsi: Europeans no longer merely check writers and France not stuck in a purely critical posture but wanting to impose a newly impartial image—this is realism we haven't seen before. Because we still have this image of a French Arab policy, looking like a stubborn legacy of history. This image remains very much present in your ministry, more at the level of reflex than of analysis.

VÉDRINE: This image is a bit out of date, if you look at our current relations with all the actors. That said, who can claim impartiality? The United States is not impartial. A more reasonable objective is to be able to speak in confidence and usefully with everybody. As for our "Arab policy," this is a sort of catch-all expression that has always been inappropriate. But it is legitimate to develop an ambitious policy with the Arab countries in all their diversity. The prime minister said this clearly in the National Assembly after his trip to Israel and the Palestinian territories in February 2000.

MOÏSI: Washington used to complain about France's Arab policy by talking about three things: oil, arms sales, and for the more sophisticated, the number of countries that would vote with France at the UN in one circumstance or another.

VÉDRINE: As if oil, arms sales, and UN votes didn't play a role in American policies! This critique says more about the way the Americans view the world than it does about France's Arab policy. It wouldn't be too difficult, in fact, to identify the names of the companies or the senators or representatives whose interests have been behind many American political and diplomatic initiatives in the region. This does not represent the constructive spirit in which we now cooperate with U.S. foreign policy toward the Middle East peace process.

MOÏSI: What, specifically, does France bring to these issues? A small but significant contribution that we alone can make on the issues of Lebanon and Syria and our ideas on the Israel-Palestinian peace process?

VÉDRINE: "A small contribution"? You're understating what we can bring. If you look at what people expect from us—the French president and government—at the requests we get, you will see that our contribution must be real and large. I already mentioned the role that France played in enlightening others from the beginning of the 1980s until the end of the 1990s. Everything France called for, from mutual recognition to the creation of a Palestinian state, was courageous! France was the first Western country to stand up for these things. And we have not stopped since to bring real added value through our work as facilitators, on the Israel-Palestinian track as well as on the Syrian and Lebanese tracks. It is thanks to my predecessor that in 1996 a consultative group was set up to observe the South Lebanon Agreement and that France became a co-president. In fall 1999, France helped to convince Damascus and Tel Aviv to resume their negotiations—which later broke down. Today we're developing French-Israeli bilateral ties, but we also emphasize the fact that the Palestinian state must be viable, which the Israeli proposals didn't yet allow for. And now in the Security Council we're examining the consequences of the Israeli retreat from South Lebanon—what can and must be done so that Resolution 425 is applied in the right conditions—so that the situation that emerges is stable and there is security for everyone. We're looking at what can be done to get the Israel-Syria dialogue going again.

MOÏSI: Does Europe allow us to get beyond whatever might remain from the old Franco-British colonial rivalries?

VÉDRINE: They are long gone. And anyway, what would they be about? In the Middle East, just as in Africa, we no longer have rivalries or contradictions, just different memories or particularities sometimes, but these are fading.

MOÏSI: Does Europe also help us get beyond the different orientations of a country like Germany, whose history leads it to have a special relationship with Israel, and a country like France, which sees itself as more "neutral" or "objective" in debates about the Middle East?

VÉDRINE: These different orientations no longer prevent a common European approach. But if you were to take away from Europe today the contributions of French and British policy, those of Italian, Spanish, or Greek foreign policy, what would remain of its positions on the Middle East? Communiqués approving of peace deals, or criticizing obstacles to their implementation or violations, and financial aid when things go well. In other words, a combination of a well-intentioned nongovernmental organization (NGO) and a big regional bank for peaceful development! This is no longer enough. The political approach of the European Union is almost always organized around the action of two or three countries and the tenacious work of our special envoy, Miguel Angel Moratinos.

Moïsi: The Palestinians used to see us essentially as a means by which to pressure the United States. They weren't able to talk to Washington directly and used Europe not so much because they cared what Europe had to say but because of the possible influence of the European line on Washington. Is this still the case? Or have we managed to convince the Arabs that what we had to say was important in itself and not just because of who we were, and to convince Washington that our role wasn't negative but complementary? Does the U.S. Congress see it this way, and has the American Jewish community begun to do so?

Védrine: Not Congress. Its world view does not lead it to accept the idea of complementarity! The American Jewish community accepts this more than before. The Arabs do. The Israelis, too. We have rebuilt a situation in which we are no longer used by anyone, in which we can no longer be considered the extension of anyone else's influence. We are what we are: France, Europe. It is a more dignified and more respectable position, and ultimately, more effective.

Moïsi: The European special envoy to the Middle East, Mr. Moratinos, the excellent Spanish diplomat you referred to, conducts with modesty and perseverance a policy that is discreet but not unimportant. Could the Solana-Moratinos duo one day play an even more significant role?

Védrine: The stronger the cohesion of the union and the more our proposals have to contribute, the more the EU's special envoys will be listened to.

Moïsi: Are there any other purely French approaches to the Middle East?

Védrine: Yes. On Iraq, we think that the legitimate security aspirations of Iraq's neighbors can be ensured without continuing to rely on the embargo that penalizes—very cruelly—the population, even as it is manipulated by the leaders. Resolution 1284 should allow us to make progress in this direction. On Iran, we were the first, along with Italy, to think that it was worth responding positively to the signals of openness from President Khatami, without thereby forgetting that the "reformers" are a branch of the Islamic revolution.

Moïsi: What about on the Arab-Israeli peace process? Europe and the United States worked together but failed to bring about peace. Did you ever think an agreement was possible?

Védrine: From the end of Camp David in July 2000 until Ariel Sharon's provocative visit to the Temple Mount at the end of September, and then again with President Clinton's late-December framework proposals, yes, I really did think we were closer than ever to a solution.

Moïsi: Why?

Védrine: First, because Israeli prime minister Ehud Barak had been elected to make peace. On Jerusalem and the Palestinian territories he had put forward the most advanced proposals ever made by an Israeli government. Of course, according to international law, Israel should purely and simply have handed over all the occupied territories. But in the real world that we live in, the proposals of Barak and Foreign Minister Shlomo Ben Ami were very courageous.

Moïsi: The Palestinians were not so courageous.

Védrine: You can't say that. They also showed unprecedented flexibility, on the territories and settlements. They stuck to their demands on Jerusalem and refugees. You've got to understand that it is a tremendous responsibility for a Palestinian leader to tell his people that the historic struggle is over and that the agreement is definitive, especially in the absence of complete and immediate resolution of all the essential issues.

Moïsi: What was Bill Clinton's role?

Védrine: It was essential and extraordinary. He committed himself more than any previous president. He did this with all the power of the American presidency, but also with the personal magnetism toward the other leaders that he had built up over his many meetings with them. This also derived from a certain rebalancing of the American position and Clinton's personal charm. Madeleine Albright was also incredibly active.

I regret that all this did not succeed, but hope that something of it will endure.

Moïsi: Europe, on the other hand, didn't play much of a role.

Védrine: Europe, as such, has so far not played a true political role in the Middle East. Thus everything it has been doing over the past several years—with its financial aid, its cooperation programs, its special envoy, Mr. Moratinos, the activity of its high representative for foreign policy, its increasingly precise and firm declarations on Middle East peace—constitute progress and increased influence.

Moïsi: But we cannot be content with so little!

Védrine: I agree. We must be much more ambitious. The EU cannot limit itself to expressing nice words, giving out humanitarian aid, and sending envoys to the region. It needs a real policy. With Spain and some other countries, France continually pushes for this.

Moïsi: Which runs the risk of antagonism with the United States.

Védrine: Why should that be? We can have our own ideas and usefully cooperate with the Americans for peace in the Middle East. But Europe also needs the courage to take up its responsibilities and take positions that it judges to be right for peace. It should refuse to be disqualified in advance by Israel or the United States, or instrumentalized by the Arabs.

Moïsi: The United States often judges France's Arab policy harshly, pointing to its partiality and commercial ulterior motives.

Védrine: Please, don't make me laugh: commercial considerations play no role in American foreign policy, do they? More seriously, commercial factors play a certain role in all foreign policies. In France's case, they are not dominant, especially in the Middle East, where our reasoning is strategic.

Moïsi: Can you be more precise?

Védrine: France has been saying for twenty years that a viable Palestinian state is the *solution,* not the *problem,* and thus that the Israelis and the Palestinians must agree to accept each other and to negotiate. These ideas were caricatured and strongly resisted for years (remember the virulent attacks on François Mitterrand when he received Yassir Arafat, before Arafat had become a regular at the White House), before ultimately coming to be seen as the obvious basis from which to work, by Americans as well as Israelis! There is an example of our having a real influence on the evolution of attitudes, even though we did not have the unique position that the United States has for decades had in the Middle East in the eyes of the Arabs and the Palestinians.

Moïsi: Has anything changed in France's relations with the United States in the Middle East?

Védrine: Yes, under Bill Clinton we replaced the sterile and suspicious climate of mutual reproach with a very active cooperation, extensive exchange of information, and even, in certain cases—such as on Lebanon and Syria—a true operational coordination on the position to adopt and the steps to take. All this while respecting our own specificity. I hope this will continue under George W. Bush.

Moïsi: Was there true cooperation?

Védrine: Yes, for example, during the summer of 2000, on the search for an Israeli-Palestinian agreement, with constant exchanges of papers and telephone conversations.

Moïsi: But it didn't work. Is this because the Palestinians have, once again, missed the boat?

Védrine: You can regret their reaction, as you can certain Israeli obstructions. Personally, I regret that things didn't work out overall. But let's not judge either one side or the other. Instead, let's ask what we can usefully do now.

Moïsi: Since the end of September 2000, have we not entered a new phase, in which Raymond Aron's cold war formula "impossible war, improbable peace" describes the situation in the Middle East?

Védrine: On the Middle East, I try to be neither pessimistic nor optimistic, but engaged and determined to persevere. Whatever the situa-

tion on the ground, we must not lower our guard. We must not suc-
cumb to the fatalism of this formula, nor content ourselves with something in between.

Moïsi: So what can we do?

Védrine: You've got to distinguish between our role and the parties'
role. In the end, only the Israelis and Palestinians will be able to make
the historic decisions—necessarily very difficult because they will
require concessions and compromises—that will be the foundation for
the peace that will have to be built on them. What can the others, the
United States and Europe, do? Advise, deter, encourage, propose, help,
and guarantee. Accompany, and thus facilitate. They cannot substitute
for the protagonists.

Moïsi: Yes, but concretely?

Védrine: Today, we can promote the lessening of tensions on the
ground, see what can be preserved from the political and diplomatic
agreements of the past few months, help to restart the negotiations by
providing some perspective, and see what we can get going between
Israelis and Palestinians, and Israelis and Syrians—all while making
sure the legitimate interests of the Lebanese and Jordanians are not
neglected. We need to seek the best possible synergy among Americans, Europeans, and Egyptians. And never despair.

Moïsi: What would you say to the Israelis and the Palestinians?

Védrine: To the former, I would say: Overcome your fears. The existence of Israel is both a given and an inalienable right. Understand the
despair and the expectations of the Palestinians. Take radical and
courageous steps. Go to the end of the logic of peace: you need a genuinely viable Palestinian state.

To the Palestinians, I would say: Understand the particular concerns of the Israelis, and thus their deep need for security. Some day
you will need to choose between an absolute vision of what is just and
what you are due and the reality of what will be possible. I understand
that you wanted to make more possible and I can feel the suffering and
even the despair, but this choice will have to be made one day or
another.

The entire world will help the Israeli and Palestinian leaders who, together, have shown this courage.

MOÏSI: Are there, aside from Africa and the Middle East, other foreign policy areas that would seem to you legitimately to have something specifically French about them?

VÉDRINE: This is not the right way to look at the issue. France has legitimate interests everywhere, more or less important, but real—because it is present in this or that region of the world through its overseas departments or territories; because of its historic relations with this or that country; because it has global responsibilities as a member of the UN Security Council or the G-7/G-8; or because of a French tradition of making proposals about the organization of the world that goes back at least to the post–World War I period, even before the League of Nations. This tradition played an essential role in 1945–46 and remains alive. We have, on all subjects, our analyses and views of the solutions that should be proposed, whether it's helping Russia transform itself from the ruins of the Soviet Union into a big, modern, democratic, and peaceful country, or tackling Asia's many problems, be they in North Asia, Indonesia, or on India-Pakistan relations, not to mention the many other subjects we have been talking about.

MOÏSI: Would the foreign minister of any other member state of the European Union be able to speak like you just did, stressing the national contribution and striking such a balance in the same terms? Could Joschka Fischer have spoken like that? Would even Robin Cook have spoken like this?

VÉDRINE: Robin Cook or Tony Blair can certainly talk like this. And, as a matter of fact, they do! German leaders, too, in their own way, but what's more is that they act this way. And lots of other European ministers think and act like this in situations where they have direct interests. They look for the right combination between the national level and the European level. None of them, I continually note, thinks there's anything out of date about it.

MOÏSI: Though they don't dare speak out like you do.

VÉDRINE: Sure they do! Some may prefer to formulate their position subject by subject, rather than in a comprehensive way. Other ministers don't think this way because their country doesn't have the same traditions in foreign policy, and then there is the case of Chancellor Schroeder's Germany, which expresses itself normally—the end of the war was more than a half-century ago! Germany could speak louder without anyone becoming concerned. It defends its interests very well.

MOÏSI: The difference is thus not between the Bonn Republic and the Berlin Republic, between the divided Germany and the united Germany, but in your view it's a question of temperaments, personalities, circumstances?

VÉDRINE: Of course, I don't underestimate how important 1989–90 was. Remember Helmut Kohl calling for Croatian independence, rapid European enlargement, etc. But to get to the heart of your question, I would say that all European leaders, without exception, seek to combine as well as possible the always present national interest and the growing European interest. They believe they are succeeding and they do not see any insurmountable contradiction in this. It is in this way, I am certain, that we will get beyond the next stages, notably in the area of the CFSP, as demonstrated by the increasingly well-coordinated action of the EU countries in Bosnia, Croatia, Kosovo, and the whole of the Balkans. Each country of the union contributes in its own way, but together, on all the subjects that in the past would have exacerbated our differences.

MOÏSI: What is the future of the CFSP?

VÉDRINE: In my view, national foreign policies that remain distinct but are increasingly convergent. They will be increasingly harmonized within a general European body of doctrine, but with several countries playing the role of motor. There will be common strategies and common actions when there is European consensus, incarnated or expressed by Mr. CFSP. In defense policy, there will be a true intervention capability for crises on Europe's periphery, to be used in cases when, unfortunately, this should prove indispensable.

Ethics and Realism

DOMINIQUE MOÏSI: Are we in the process of experiencing a political-moral revolution in this era of globalization? Notwithstanding tragedies like Chechnya, is a true international morality—human rights—about to take hold, replacing concepts like raison d'état and the idea that the end justifies the means?

HUBERT VÉDRINE: It's not so simple. The meaning of raison d'état shouldn't be presented so schematically. As for the aspiration to democracy, it is indeed continuing to get stronger. Some talk about a new paradigm. Can it become a universal one, other than on the surface? This is desirable, but to know, you can't only look at the world from a Western point of view. Let's not forget that what we call human rights—those that were codified in the twentieth century in international texts and which serve as a reference point for our value judgements (and thus for our condemnations)—were formulated in the second half of the eighteenth century by the Americans, the French, the English, in Philadelphia, Paris, or London. They were then taken to the ends of the earth by a Europe that sometimes was an emancipator but more often was expansionist and colonialist. For some, this still colors perceptions.

Moïsi: That doesn't mean that they do not constitute progress or that they are not universal!

Védrine: No, of course not, and this in no way diminishes our attachment to these principles. But it does explain a still perceptible ambivalence among all the non-Westerners, who constitute, let's not forget, five-sixths of humanity. In a growing part of the world, people do want more and more democracy—and this is a good thing—but not necessarily ours, exactly as it is. Finally, let's not forget that these rights were introduced by colonizers—missionaries, administrators, soldiers—who proclaimed them without always applying them, and that today it is the mighty who are always demanding that these rights be respected.

Moïsi: Aren't all these considerations out of date today? With his cultural relativism, doesn't Samuel Huntington confuse culture and political culture? Why shouldn't Singaporeans, for example, have comparable democratic aspirations to ours? Why wouldn't the Chinese have the right to democracy?

Védrine: Of course they do. But the question that Western diplomats have to deal with is not that one. It is to know what can usefully be done *from the outside.*

Moïsi: But the movement toward democracy is universal!

Védrine: Sure, but it will be all the more universal if it is not seen only as a forced Westernization or an Americanization. Otherwise, the risks of rejection out of concerns for identity are inevitable. Let's try to avoid them!

Let's look back a bit. Since President Wilson's "war aims," proclaimed January 8, 1918, the West has again become a proselytizer. I say "again" somewhat tongue in cheek, thinking of Pope Urban II, the "inventor" (in 1095 in Clermont-Ferrand) of the first crusade—and thus of the "right to intervene"—when it goes off course! This is Wilsonianism before Wilson! The West stops proselytizing after the collapse of the League of Nations, the stagnation of the 1920s and

1930s, and the horrors of World War II. It starts up again with the Atlantic Charter, signed in 1941 by Franklin D. Roosevelt and Winston Churchill. After the war, in 1945, it inspires the Charter of the United Nations: "We the peoples of the United Nations determined . . . to live together in peace with one another as good neighbors . . . ." But this momentum is immediately halted by the cold war and the Russian veto, which paralyze the Security Council and smother the utopia in its embryonic stage. It resumes, however, four decades later with the collapse of the U.S.S.R. in 1991, which leaves the West in charge, anxious to extend its law immediately and uncompromisingly to the rest of the world. The imposition of human rights from the outside has since become *the* raison d'être of a determined ideological movement that thinks it can toss centuries of diplomacy, that is to say, the search for peace, into the closet. This is what explains the outbreak of debates about boycotts and other kinds of sanctions, ideal weapons for those who want to rule from a distance without risk to themselves. The universalization of values and Western hubris sometimes go hand in hand.

Moïsi: But why should we put off the founding of democracy, wherever it may be?

Védrine: It's not a question of putting it off, but rather of seeing how it can advance. If we had in our possession a recipe for instant democracy that could be applied anywhere, it would be unforgivable if we didn't immediately allow people to take advantage of it. But do we have it? Just as the relativist thesis—that the Chinese or the Africans are not "made for" democracy—is of course inadmissible, the question of the pace and sequence of the process is essential. Yet we refuse to admit this. Didn't it take us two or three centuries to build our own democracies, which are, in any case, far from perfect in the United States as well as in Europe? One hundred and fifty years, for example, for France to go from the first elections, in 1795, to female suffrage in 1945! How can we take a magic wand and suddenly make China into a big Singapore, Russia into a big Sweden, and the Balkans into Switzerland? How can we get Afghanistan, Somalia, and the African states of the Great Lakes region out of the vicious circle? We would all like that to go more quickly, but no one knows the short cut, the little door from *Alice in*

Wonderland. Thus you have to go through processes. How can they be accelerated? This is the question, and it's what our policy is all about.

Moïsi: At least it is possible to be clear about the principles.

Védrine: This goes without saying. So long as we don't just stop there or think this means that we don't have to change mentalities or encourage the development of the rule of law. Let me repeat: the difficulty is not in the proclamation of the universality of the principles—nothing could be easier!—but in the Western origin of those who prescribe them and in the way that we demand their application from the outside.

Moïsi: You think we're on the wrong track, that we're playing with fire?

Védrine: I think that the goal is the right one but the method is sometimes wrong.

Moïsi: How so?

Védrine: First of all, the risk of arrogance and the reactions that it provokes. Having finally settled down after centuries of cruel history, intra-European wars, colonial wars, and then world wars, we forget all this and look down on others—making demands, condemning, and sanctioning. Is this legitimate? Everything depends on who this "we" is. But the real question is, does it work? The answer is that it depends on the case at hand, the timing, the context, and many other factors. Sure, we're so strong, so rich, so influential, and so threatening that we manage to get others around the world to accept at least a superficial layer of democracy, "Potemkin democracy." But can it take root? Depending on whether we think democratization is a process or a conversion, the policies to be followed are very different.

Moïsi: What do you mean by that?

Védrine: A conversion is instantaneous, a revelation. A process takes time. For me it's clear: linked positively or negatively to the countries in question and the regional context, democratization results first of all from an internal economic, cultural, social, and thus political process that needs to be accelerated. But it is nonetheless a process, with stages. To stimulate it, and help it along, in general it's better to encourage than to penalize. To demand perfect democracy is to think in religious terms, as if you're waiting for a revelation like the one that knocked St. Paul off his horse, to convert tyrants into zealots of democracy. If you think like this, dogmatically, you are logically led to think only in terms of sanctions, punishments, and excommunications. This is not the way I look at it.

Moïsi: Isn't there, in the way you look at things, a danger of "realism until the bitter end" that justifies anything, including the worst?

Védrine: Excess is always a vice! There is realism and realism. It is fatalism that resigns itself to everything and justifies everything, not realism, which is the condition of all effective action. In this case, realism consists, more than anything, of admitting that, beyond its formalistic aspects, democracy cannot survive if people are hungry, afraid, and illiterate, if their most basic vital rights are flouted, and if the state they live in is incapable of carrying out its basic functions. The secretary general of the United Nations Conference on Trade and Development (UNCTAD), the Brazilian Rubens Ricupero, estimates that the richest people in the world now earn around 150 times more than the poorest; he sees globalization as a system that sidelines 5 billion human beings. The World Bank underlines the worsening of poverty. There is no point in sticking transparent and pluralist elections onto this situation just in order to feel better, without trying, in most cases, to do something about it. They will never take.

Moïsi: So what should we do?

Védrine: Tighten up the link between development and democratization, which doesn't happen automatically. Develop for each particular case a mix—or maybe I should say a "protocol," to use the language of therapy—of incentives, encouragement, conditions, and a schedule—slow or fast—adapted to each situation and each country. Limiting yourself to making official note of each violation of human rights and condemning it is not enough. You've got to be more ambitious, more engaged, thus more up to speed on the realities and the potential for change in each situation.

Moïsi: I would like to take some concrete cases and talk about certain offensive diplomatic contacts. Is it now acceptable and necessary to meet with everyone? A large part of public opinion no longer accepts that we should greet tyrants, despots, or authoritarian leaders with pomp and circumstance in the name of realism.

VÉDRINE: Without wanting to be too provocative, let me say that for us Europeans, foreign policy is reduced to mere decorum if it's just a question of getting together with your friends or "respectable" people who think like us. We might as well give up right away on working on any problems or resolving any crises and just let the United States—which doesn't shy away from anything—run everything. We would be such purists that we'd end up abandoning any attempt to influence events.

MOÏSI: Still, can we fraternize with just anyone?

VÉDRINE: Of course not! But who's talking about fraternizing? It's a question of resolving problems that come up between states, whatever they may be. To be sure, through the affirmation of our "values," a more militant, law-dispensing, and willingly Manichaean conception is starting to emerge today. Is the role of foreign policy to resolve problems—involving all the relevant actors—or to encourage the spread of democracy everywhere? I don't think these two approaches should be seen as alternatives and I'm working to find a dynamic synthesis of them, from above.

MOÏSI: You yourself backed a policy of "warning" and "vigilance" toward the Austrian government formed in February 2000.

VÉDRINE: Yes, I was even the first to say, starting in October 1999, that Austria would be putting itself in a deplorable situation if it succumbed to the temptation of a coalition government with the extreme right, and I was the first to denounce the politicians over there who exploit the real or supposed fears of the population. By deciding, by means of a referendum in 1994, to enter Europe, Austria subscribed to its program and to its democratic values—Article 6 of the treaty, which confers upon European Union (EU) members the right to warn, to try to deter, to oversee, and even to sanction "serious and repeated" violations of the principles guaranteed by the EU treaties. We have the right to protect ourselves against ideas that go against our convictions. There is, of course, no relation between today's Europe and that of the 1930s; the comparisons are unfounded. But the risks of xenophobia are, on the other hand, quite real, given the strong migration pressures. These risks must be taken quite seriously and cut off. Policies that exploit them must be condemned, though we must also avoid policies that, out of naïve optimism, exacerbate them. The European measures taken against Austria were lifted after a group of three "wise men" noted that they had had positive effects. And at Nice the fifteen improved their system of early vigilance and warning.

Moïsi: Isn't it sort of hypocritical to behave like we did toward Austria while we put out the red carpet for China? Does Europe's democratic identity justify this double standard?

Védrine: Let us repeat that entering the European Union brings with it particular commitments. And should we insult the Chinese? China was condemned for a number of years by the UN Commission on Human Rights in Geneva. The result? Nothing. Can we really think that the evolution of the world in and of itself that is China, with its 1.2 billion inhabitants, is going to skip some stages because it was condemned by Western capitals? Everything we know about China and about the development of democracy suggests otherwise, so much so that in 1997, 1998, and 1999, the EU preferred a critical political dialogue to condemnation.

Moïsi: But did this more realistic approach lead to concrete results? Did it encourage China to show more moderation and openness?

Védrine: No, and that's the problem! We can point to the fact that China signed two UN agreements on political, economic, and social rights. But it has not ratified them yet. When he came to Europe in 1999, President Xiang Zemin made no further commitments. However, by confirming their desire to enter the WTO, Chinese leaders created for themselves a commitment to economic, and thus eventually political, modernization. I suppose they're conscious of this. In any case, for these reasons, in 2000 the union was ready to vote for a more critical text, but the majority of the member states of the Human Rights Commission did not want a vote.

Moïsi: The American position toward China is at least as ambiguous as Europe's?

Védrine: Yes. Because of its ties to Taiwan and Hollywood's engagement on behalf of Tibet, the Clinton administration was often very critical of Beijing. At the same time, it viewed China as a strategic partner and supported China's desire to join the WTO.

Moïsi: Do you think the new administration will have a very different policy?

Védrine: Colin Powell questions China's status as a strategic partner. We shall see how and in what proportions the new administration combines cooperation and confrontation.

Moïsi: What's your own view of China's evolution?

Védrine: I believe China will inevitably change; that the growing wealth of the country will generate a request, then a demand, for political liberalism and democracy; that the pressure exerted in this direction will be formidable; that the current leaders are trying to put off this development, while at the same time preparing for it, in effect by doing things in the reverse order from that followed by Mikhail Gorbachev for his own country. At the end of the day, can the Beijing regime transform itself politically? This is not a given.

Moïsi: But in that case, we can't do anything other than wait patiently and try to promote our interests?

Védrine: There are always things we can do! In this particular case, we shouldn't forget that everything about Chinese nationalism and then communism reflected China's desire to regain respect. In my view, China—even more than any other proud and long-humiliated country—will rebel against any form of outside interference that will remind it of the unequal treaties that were imposed on it at a time of weakness, the Open Door policy, or Japanese imperialism. China will change, first of all, through its ambition to be one of the key actors in a multipolar world. And it will change under the pressure of the Chinese themselves—for example, under the effect of the concessions they made to enter the WTO and, to take a concrete example, following the proliferation of mobile phones. We should encourage and promote this tendency; but we are not in a position to impose it. Europe's stance at the Human Rights Commission in Geneva in April 2000, that it was prepared to vote for a resolution criticizing China for the absence of progress in the area of human rights, expressed disappointment and was a valuable signal.

Moïsi: Let's turn to Russia. What positions should the EU and France adopt toward Putin's Russia? Putin seems to embody all of Russia and the Soviet Union's legacy of the twentieth century. He seems to be most driven by his intense and sincere nationalism. What does that mean for Europeans? Can we judge Russia on anything other than its actions, and according to what criteria, ours or those that we judge to be better adapted to today's Russia? In other words, does the need for stability and order require a certain flexibility in the application of democratic principles?

Védrine: Let's first take note that no other country has had to build a society, economy, and modern democracy on the equivalent of the ruins of the former U.S.S.R., following decades of despotism! Our objective and interest are clear: a democratic, prosperous, and pacific Russia. But how to get there, how quickly, and what would we do in Putin's place? None of this is obvious. Thus it is no use comparing contemporary Western democratic criteria to the true state of Russia and being shocked every morning. Let's instead ask how we can have a useful influence on Russia's political and economic evolution from the outside. When I went to see Putin in February 2000, he told me he wanted "to bring Russian legislation closer to European legislation." France, during its European presidency, promoted the reorientation of European cooperation with Russia toward the reinforcement of the *état de droit*—a state based on the rule of law. In the phrase *état de droit* there is the law (*droit*), but also the state (*état*). We should admit that Russia, like all countries, needs to be governed.

Moïsi: Doesn't this view open the door to all sorts of abuses?

Védrine: Many of the abuses of these past few years were due to the absence of a state deserving of the name. The state we're talking about should be a modern, democratic, and regulating *état de droit*, which has never existed in Russia. Let us thus support Vladimir Putin's policies that go in this direction, while pointing out clearly to him in advance the unacceptable regressions.

Moïsi: Putin's Russia is trying to recover a national identity through the reaffirmation of a specific international role and a foreign policy it can be proud of. Does this mean that we should overlook the unacceptable violations of human rights in Chechnya, in the name of a certain kind of realism, or that we'll only condemn these violations as a matter of principle?

Védrine: You are right about the sources of this nationalism and patriotism: overcoming the humiliation of the past decade, being respected, becoming a great power once again. Our policy should seek to make Russia understand that its new foreign policy must remain compatible with what Moscow, at the same time, expects from Europe and the United States in what Russia calls its "near abroad," as well as elsewhere. Where Chechnya is concerned, when you say that "we condemn as a matter of principle," let me remind you that France was the Western country that in winter 1999–2000 most clearly condemned the terrible effects of the Chechen war on civilians and told Russia that it was seriously losing its way. What did others say? Moreover, the difference you claim to see between our realism and principles disappears when you ask what we can do that will be useful, beyond protests. How can we speed up the moment when Russia will understand that even from its own point of view it can no longer treat a problem like Chechnya with such purely repressive methods? We have not given up trying to convince the Russians of this, and I hope President Putin genuinely accelerates the search for a political solution, based on Chechen autonomy within the Russian federation.

Moïsi: The Kursk tragedy showed the limits of change in Russia where transparency is concerned. It also seems to suggest disturbing weaknesses regarding Russia's military equipment. What should we do, together with Russia and the parts of its former empire, to protect ourselves from the potential weakness of the former U.S.S.R.? Are we devoting sufficient means and attention to this?

VÉDRINE: Let's not be paternalistic about it. Before being a problem for us, it is most of all a problem for the Russians, and they're the ones who must respond. If they accept the principle of cooperation, we can work together, in the spirit of what has been done over the past few years in the area of dismantling nuclear arsenals.

Moïsi: Given Russia's situation today, should we support the requests of candidate countries for enlargement of the North Atlantic Treaty Organization (NATO), such as the Baltic states?

VÉDRINE: It is perhaps more urgent and less problematic to develop Euro-Russian structures of cooperation, for example, in the framework of the Northern Dimension that the Swedes and the Finns are encouraging the European Union to develop. Generally, I do not subscribe to the idea that we should treat Russia as a potential adversary. All the more so, in that the Baltic states are now negotiating their accession to the European Union. It seems sensible to me to seek a partnership with Russia, even if this type of relationship remains to be built.

Moïsi: Moving from the Russian question to Kosovo, can we say that NATO won the war against Serbia?

VÉDRINE: In 1999, with our political and diplomatic means truly exhausted and after the contact group had tried everything, NATO's action became inevitable. All the Europeans, members of the Alliance or not, reached the same conclusions, just like the United States. NATO's action was decisive in stopping what the Serb military forces, police, and militia were doing in Kosovo. But it was we who made use of NATO, and not the other way around.

Moïsi: What do you think of the work done since then by the UN and its special envoy, Bernard Kouchner?

VÉDRINE: The international community has done all it can to build a democratic and substantially autonomous Kosovo. For the UN, the United Nations Mission in Kosovo (UNMIK), with Kouchner in charge, did an exceptional job, managing more than 4,000 police and military officers (including 79 French), and nearly 4,000 civilian officials and local recruits. The Kosovo Force (KFOR) did the same for

NATO, the Stability Pact for the EU (with a budget commitment of 1.8 billion euros), and the Organization for Security and Cooperation in Europe (OSCE) for elections. Having said that, we still have a tough job ahead of us. Long-term engagement will be necessary to create in Kosovo the structures and mentalities required to promote coexistence among the Kosovars, Serbs, and others. In this sense, the peaceful holding of municipal elections in October 2000 was a remarkable success, thanks notably to Bernard Kouchner. The victory of Ibrahim Rugova's "moderates" was good news for Kosovo and our democratic ambitions.

Moïsi: Paradoxically, over the past few months the good news seems to have been coming from Belgrade! The peaceful transition from Slobodan Milosevic to Vojislav Kostunica in Serbia is something of a divine surprise—how do you explain it? Did the European Union play a decisive role by providing hope for Serbs desperate for "normality"?

Védrine: Well before the September 2000 elections in Serbia, twelve out of the fifteen countries of the EU wanted to lift sanctions against Serbia (except for those on Milosevic and his top officials), because we judged them to be counterproductive. When the Serbian democratic opposition decided to meet Milosevic's electoral challenge, as president of the general affairs council, I proposed this to our fourteen partners, who accepted the strategy of turning these dubious and cumbersome sanctions into a mechanism for change.

Moïsi: In what sense?

Védrine: By promising, in a message to the Serbian people in early September, that sanctions would be lifted if there was a democratic victory. This victory was that of the Serbian people and the democratic opposition, but President Kostunica told me five days after his victory that the appeal had an encouraging and decisive effect.

Moïsi: It is nonetheless the case that Kostunica's nationalism is at least as vigorous and intense as Milosevic's! How do you respond to those who dream of reconstituting Yugoslavia, at least with Kosovo and Montenegro, as if nothing had happened? And what do you say to the Albanians, who see no alternative to full and complete independence?

VÉDRINE: President Kostunica defines himself as a nationalist, but moderate and democratic. And he has already begun to prove it. After his astonishing electoral victory in September, we talked within the EU and agreed that at this point our priority was not to overwhelm him with demands and conditions, but to consolidate democracy and thus to help him win the legislative elections of December 23, which he did. We now need to act together toward Serbia, Montenegro, and Kosovo so that the new Serb and Yugoslav leaders put forward inventive institutional proposals, and the Montenegrins, on the one hand, and the Kosovars on the other, agree to discuss them, all while respecting UN Security Council Resolution 1244. Their common desire to tighten their links to the EU obliges them to demonstrate their sense of responsibility. In Kosovo itself, we must work to create all the political and security conditions that should make it possible to hold elections for the autonomous assembly in 2001. We have to create a new dynamic that makes it possible to solve the problems of coexistence that today seem insoluble. That's what it means to "Europeanize the Balkans."

MOÏSI: Does Europe have the means to carry out peacekeeping tasks in Kosovo and Bosnia-Herzegovina by itself if the American troops leave, as George W. Bush's national security adviser, Condoleezza Rice, suggested during the American presidential campaign?

VÉDRINE: First of all, the military dimension is only one aspect of our policy in the Balkans. More broadly, at its summit in Zagreb in November 2000, the EU proposed a stabilization and association process for the Balkan countries in the coming years and encouraged them to cooperate regionally. As for peacekeeping, it's up to the new American administration to decide what it wants to participate in, and at what level. The Europeans, who have in less than two years built up the structures of European defense, have no particular need to worry about having to play a greater role, which would be paradoxical. Nonetheless, it would be preferable for the United States to continue upholding its commitments alongside the Europeans in the Balkans.

MOÏSI: What was the impact of the Kosovo war on our relations with Russia? Should we see it as having a lasting impact or was it just an episode?

VÉDRINE: The impact was momentarily negative. Boris Yeltsin took it very badly, even though he had no sympathy for Milosevic. He was angry at the Europeans, but on the basis of a misinterpretation of what was happening. In any case, the Russians had to be realistic and take the Western point of view on Kosovo and Serbia into account, and all this is now behind us, with Kostunica's coming to power. On our side, we must do all we can so that Russia is associated as closely as possible with all our policy in the Balkans, via the UN Security Council, the contact group, or the G-8. This is in all of Europe's interest.

MOÏSI: Since Kostunica's coming to power in Serbia, the question of international justice for war criminals has become even more acute. Do you feel that justice and the need to remember are conditions of peace and eventual reconciliation, or can the insistence on justice, on the contrary, paradoxically lead to the return of violence and ethnic divisions? What, in your view, should be the international community's role in this difficult area?

VÉDRINE: The fight against impunity is essential. If national judicial systems do not work, justice must be done at the international level, which will be the role of the International Criminal Court. The Federal Republic of Yugoslavia has obligations toward the Hague Tribunal. But I can understand why President Kostunica is proceeding slowly—he has said that trying Milosevic is not his highest priority. He contests the legitimacy of the International Criminal Court but is not refusing to cooperate with it. I think Serbian public opinion will gradually evolve, as it starts to become aware of Milosevic's crimes. A "truth and reconciliation commission" could help with this process. As for ethnic coexistence in this region, the political work must go ahead, because judging and resolving are not necessarily the same thing. Both are necessary.

MOÏSI: Let's come back to human rights and examine other examples, farther away, in Asia, like the case of Burma.

VÉDRINE: In Burma, an obtuse dictatorship—obsessed by the risk that this country, long torn apart by peripheral ethnic guerilla movements, will disintegrate—has put a corset on the country and relentlessly harasses Aung San Su Chi, who won the elections in 1990 and subsequently won the Nobel Peace Prize. At the initiative of Great Britain, the European Union suspended all relations with Burma. As a result, the dialogue between the EU and the Association of Southeast Asian Nations (ASEAN)—which has been very useful—was suspended. Did all this accelerate the desired changes in Burma? Nothing is less certain. I agreed in April to a reinforcement of the measures directed against the regime, on the condition that the EU-ASEAN dialogue be reopened, even with Burma present. This took place. We will not let up our pressure on the regime.

Moïsi: Indonesia?

Védrine: It was President Habibie who accepted the referendum in East Timor. The International Monetary Fund (IMF) sanctions may have contributed to this. Subsequently, the EU imposed sanctions; I won agreement that they would automatically be lifted once Jakarta had committed to applying the UN Security Council resolution on East Timor. Otherwise, we would fall back into this infernal system of indefinite sanctions which have counterproductive effects but no one dares to lift. The international intervention was not, strictly speaking, a case of interference, since Indonesia ultimately agreed to it. The situation is developing well, except that it's obviously hard for East Timor to live off its own means. On the other hand, Indonesia's future is disquieting: our encouragement of the consolidation of democracy must not reinforce its centrifugal tendencies.

Moïsi: What do you think should be done with regard to Iran?

Védrine: Since President Khatami's election, which demonstrated a desire for openness on the part of the majority of the electorate—especially among women and young people—we have encouraged this movement, in particular by receiving the Iranian president in Paris. But we remain cautious, because the opposition to this new course remains very strong in Iran.

Moïsi: There is also Iraq, which we have spoken about.

Védrine: I have said why the Security Council's objectives need to be pursued by means other than the current embargo, which is useless, cruel, and inadequate.

Moïsi: And in Africa, shouldn't we restrict our aid to the countries whose governments respect human rights, or at least to those who don't violate them too openly?

Védrine: It depends on the dynamics at work. At the end of the cold war, in an important speech at the Franco-African summit in La Baule on June 19, 1990, President François Mitterrand announced that France would henceforth give preference in its aid policies to the countries that progressed most toward democracy—without, of course, letting the others fall by the wayside, which would be the easy (and cynical) way out! At the second most recent renegotiation of the Lomé accords, in 1995, France had a procedure introduced called Article 366 *bis*, which can lead to the suspension of cooperation in the case of a coup d'état. It has already been used four times. Lionel Jospin has proven very vigilant in this area since 1997. For his part, the president of the republic congratulated the Organization of African Unity (OAU) for having committed itself in 1999 to no longer invite to its meetings leaders who came to power by coups d'état. The association agreements that the European Union signs now include a clause saying that "relations between the parties are based on respect for democratic principles and human rights." The text adopted at the Euro-African summit of April 3, 2000, stipulates that "democratization, development and the protection of fundamental freedoms and human rights are interrelated and reinforce each other." We are being careful, as we implement this new policy, not to provide "moral" alibis for a reduction in cooperation aid!

Moïsi: We saw Congolese president Laurent Kabila in Paris. Many found his presence at the November 1998 France-Africa summit offensive. Shouldn't representatives from nondemocratic governments be banned from Franco-African or Francophone summits, as is the case for the Commonwealth?

Védrine: In the Commonwealth, only Nigeria was, for a while, suspended. Afterwards, let me repeat, if you want to deal with conflicts and resolve them, you've got to talk to all the actors. How can anyone seriously try to solve the conflict in the African Great Lakes region, for example, without talking to the leaders of the Democratic Republic of Congo (DRC), Museveni, Kagame, the Congolese rebels, even in Paris,

if this is useful? That's why Charles Josselin, France's minister for cooperation, has gone several times to every country in the region. Belgian
foreign policy, which places high priority on human rights, is no different. Let's be careful not to become "moral" countries with "clean hands"
only because our hands are no longer involved. At the Europe-Africa
summit in Cairo in April 2000, Kabila, Qadaffi, Museveni, and many
others were present.

Moïsi: We spoke about international justice where Yugoslavia was
concerned. Do you think that there is, all things considered, a
"Pinochet effect" following the Chilean dictator's arrest in England,
and that this effect is a positive one?

Védrine: There will certainly be a Pinochet effect. Strictly speaking,
the only bodies that merit the name "international justice" are the two
tribunals created by the UN Security Council for former Yugoslavia
and Rwanda, and the future International Criminal Court, whose
statute was adopted, thanks in large part to the French government, in
July 1998. It will come into effect after having been ratified by sixty
countries (twenty-four, including France, have already done so). The
legal proceedings against Pinochet were launched by a Spanish judge;
those targeting a Mauritanian officer accused of torture, by a French
judge; those targeting the former Chadian president, Hissène Habré,
by a Senegalese judge, etc. What we're talking about in these cases, on
the basis of the 1981 convention against torture, is *transnational* justice,
where a national judge exercises universal jurisdiction.

Any progress in the fight against the impunity of torturers or war
criminals is important, first and foremost from the point of view of the
victims. But this type of action also needs to take into account the problem of how to end dictatorships, which rarely happens through judicial
rulings. This is what led Felipe Gonzales, who played a historic role in
the democratic transitions in Latin America, to declare, regarding
Pinochet, that "Spain has not had the right to be the judge in its former
colonies for 180 years."

Moïsi: But what do you, personally, think? Are you, like Henry
Kissinger, extremely reticent about these new forms of questioning

national sovereignty? Do you think they break down too many rules or that they can be destabilizing?

VÉDRINE: States can take the sovereign decision to delegate judicial powers to an international tribunal. That's what they have done with the International Criminal Court to judge the greatest crimes, because national judiciaries may sometimes fail to do so. This is an entirely voluntary change. I also think that these new procedures create a latent threat to dictators once they lose power. This should encourage them to be less repressive. But let's be careful not to encourage them to stay in power as long as possible!

MOÏSI: A paradox. Can't these procedures have a deterrent effect?

VÉDRINE: Without doubt, in certain cases. But this will not make crime disappear any more than national judiciaries. Also, dictatorships are born from quite particular conditions. How to get rid of them remains the key question. This has always been done politically, not judicially, and justice has come later. The fight against all forms of impunity is a duty, first and foremost for the victims. But let's steer clear of the illusion that international justice, as much as or more than national justice, is going to deter everything and resolve everything. We would run the risk of great disappointment. As we've already said, the threat of punishment is not necessarily enough to deter. Punishing and resolving are not the same thing, even though the two can sometimes go together.

MOÏSI: Can you be more specific?

VÉDRINE: Some are starting to hope that international justice will be the solution to tragedies. Yet even without going back to Henri IV or to the French Third Republic's amnesty for the former Communards in 1890, it is clear that, over the decades, no country that had to get beyond a political tragedy—whether communist, fascist, or civil war—did so *initially* through justice. In 1945 it was the victors who judged the vanquished in Nuremburg or Tokyo, but after their military victory. In France the Court of Justice of the Republic that sat from 1946 to 1952 and pronounced death sentences, sentences to hard labor or to forfeiture of civic rights, did so after victory. There is no case in which the judiciary resolved the problems first. Justice was done, to be sure, but after the political solution. The ambition of the International Criminal Court is unprecedented in this regard.

MOÏSI: But justice is critically important in order for a society to achieve reconciliation, so that it may move forward. Is long-term reconciliation possible without justice, even if the need for justice and memory might, in the short term, undermine a fragile peace?

VÉDRINE: Reconciliation can result from knowing the truth, from forgiveness, from amnesty, from condemnation, from a desire to turn the page, or from a combination of all of these. Look at the cases of Russia, Poland, the Czech Republic, Hungary, Romania, Bulgaria, Spain, Portugal, Greece, Central and South America, and South Africa, among others, or again, look at the way the problem was treated in France after the Second World War. Today, there is a much stronger demand for justice and punishment in Western Europe, perhaps because time has done its work. Being so far away from its own tragedies, with the wounds largely healed, Western Europe sees these things in a much more abstract manner and seeks—retrospectively, or for others—to take a nearly perfect stance. Even in the judicial world, many are worried about these maximalist expectations, which can backfire. The judiciary system dispenses justice, which is in itself very important. Look how the Bosnian or Rwandan political problems remain, notwithstanding the important work done by the two ad hoc international tribunals. In Sierra Leone in 1999, to try to put an end to a particularly awful civil war (child soldiers amputating the limbs of other child soldiers), the adversaries had to mutually protect themselves from possible legal proceedings against them. The neighboring countries and the British resigned themselves to this agreement, for lack of any better option. Only someone who had a better way of ending this type of atrocity could criticize them. Yet even this ultrarealist agreement did not stick. And imagine if the Israelis and the Palestinians had dragged each other off to international tribunals: do you think that would have led to peace? Some wonder whether it was the indictment of Milosevic that provoked change in Serbia. Nothing is less certain. It is, moreover, written into article 16 of the statute of the International Criminal Court that in the case of contradiction between "punishing" and "resolving," the Security Council can temporarily suspend the court's proceedings.

This is clear proof that there can be a contradiction between the two! Conclusion: you can't expect more from international justice than it can deliver, which is already quite something—the fight against impunity.

There is also a risk associated with the excessive expectations that international justice brings about.

Moïsi: What risk?

Védrine: That political leaders think that the existence of an international judicial system exempts them from having to exercise their own responsibility, which is to resolve problems, or that they don't dare do so lest they get their hands dirty.

Moïsi: Can we conclude on the Pinochet case?

Védrine: The return of General Pinochet to Chile forced the country's judicial system and new leaders to confront their historic responsibilities. They seem to want to uphold them. We are encouraging them to do so. For the future, Latin America needs policies that prevent the return of the economic, social, and political tensions that led to dictatorships during the 1970s. Yet if this continent has again become democratic, it is also the least egalitarian.

Moïsi: At least, with the progress that has been made in the areas of information, communication, and transparency, no one can any longer say, like after Auschwitz, "I didn't know!" You can choose to act or not to act. But you'll know what you're doing.

Védrine: Yes, and this is critical! Having said that, since you refer back to World War II and Auschwitz, Roosevelt and Churchill didn't have to be pushed by public opinion and the media, on the contrary. It was Churchill who mobilized British public opinion, not the reverse; and it was Roosevelt who pointed U.S. opinion in the direction he wanted to take it: toward participation in the war. When they began to learn what was happening in the extermination camps, after 1941, they pursued the global fight against Hitler with an even more total determination. But they didn't have a weapon that made an immediate victory possible. This had to wait nearly four years.

Today, it's the question of democratization that is most often posed. It's not along the lines of, "I didn't know," but rather, "How to do this from the outside?" How can certain changes be made without setting off forces that could get out of control? Camus denounced the United States' failure to consider such questions when it encouraged the Budapest insurrection in 1956: "People are always too ready to expend the blood of others!" After badly calculated interventions, we need to be careful not to regret them and end up moaning, "That's not what we wanted to happen!" There are plenty of recent examples: Jimmy Carter and the Islamic revolution in Iran, Gorbachev and the consequences of *glasnost*, George Bush's call for the insurrection of the Iraqi Kurds, the arming of the Afghans . . . .

MOÏSI: Doesn't being such a "realist," or even a "sovereignist," run the risk of justifying the status quo and doing nothing for the reform of international law?

VÉDRINE: I find your question astonishing. It has nothing to do with sovereignism and everything to do with having a sense of responsibility. There is no trace of fatalism in French policy, regarding the status quo. You are talking about reform of international law, but you aren't asking me about the unfathomable injustices of globalization. France is leading the effort to make the world work according to more equitable rules. I have pointed out what Lionel Jospin said at the UN in September 1999: "The world needs rules." We are in favor of a reform of the Security Council, expanding it to twenty-four members to make it more representative of today's world (the United States initially didn't want to go beyond twenty-one members, but it seems to have moved closer to our position). The purpose of this reform would be to make the Security Council more legitimate and effective. We are also working to improve the World Trade Organization (WTO) and to reform the IMF.

MOÏSI: Fair points. But I was thinking in particular about the *droit d'ingérence* (right of humanitarian intervention) that is so dear to Bernard Kouchner.

VÉDRINE: The provisions of Chapter VII of the UN Charter, which since 1945 have given only the Security Council a legitimate right of intervention, are no longer enough. But the *droit d'ingérence* that you are talking about makes a lot of countries nervous, for who gets to intervene? Always the same ones! I think that preserving state sovereignty is appropriate. The descendants of old European nations that built their sovereignty centuries ago, and having lived through all sorts of excesses in the use of sovereignty, Europeans have decided to limit it or to exercise it jointly. They have trouble grasping what it still represents for an immense majority of member states of the UN, in terms of dignity, national identity, and protection against a globalization that is cause for concern. Let me add that, contrary to conventional wisdom, more problems result from the weakness of a certain number of the 189 member states of the UN than from their excessive strength. We've already talked about this. In particular, it's in the context of state decomposition and uncontrolled deregulation that international crime proliferates. This by no means justifies the revolting abuses or hijacking of sovereignty that certain tyrants are sometimes guilty of when they invoke it to massively repress their own citizens or those of other countries. And it does not justify the unjust use of a right of veto to paralyze the necessary authorization by the Security Council of a humanitarian intervention. To make such interventions easier, I think the recourse to the veto right at the Security Council should become as rare and as big a deal as the invocation within the EU of the Luxembourg Compromise. The temptation to go around the Security Council, via NATO for example, would be reduced by this. I have also suggested that the permanent members of the council begin a discussion among themselves on this point, to reduce abuse and to put the use of the veto into a framework.

Moïsi: Ultimately, has it not now become realistic to be moral, or is it, in your view, still moral to be a realist? Aren't you afraid of having become too attached to the past, even anachronistic, in your attachment to realpolitik?

Védrine: My sort of realism has nothing to do with your definition of realpolitik, and none of these problems would be better resolved by a "non-realpolitik." Realism against morals? Doesn't this sort of thinking assume that states and the relations among them are immoral by nature, and that you've got realpolitik on one hand and "morality" on the other? This is not the way I think. I have never come across a situation in which there was, on the one hand, a "moral" solution, and on the other a "realist" solution. It's always mixed. But maybe you're thinking of a situation that justifies the conventional meaning of realpolitik? For me, the first commandment of morality or ethics when you're in a position of responsibility is just that: being responsible. This means not doing or saying anything without having weighed all the terms of your decision or your declaration, and it means being ready to take responsibility for the consequences that may result from them. Is this anachronistic? Isn't it instead more of a necessity that we should rehabilitate? Nobody addressed this better than Max Weber, who distinguished between an ethic of conviction and an ethic of responsibility. But if you feel closer to the latter, it does not mean you have no convictions, because an authentic ethic of responsibility itself constitutes a powerful conviction. We are not faced with a simple choice between morals and realism, but with the necessity to join them together, so as to be as effective as possible in each particular case—unless we want to content ourselves with posturing or verbose declarations. But it is necessary to be more ambitious and to want to influence events. And since, when it comes to democratic or economic modernization, we don't have a magic formula that makes it possible to skip stages of development (even if ultramonetarists believe in the "big bang"), we've got to know how to stand alongside and encourage other peoples in their attempts to move forward. In my view, progress will be all the more rapid and far reaching if it proceeds from a dialectic between external encouragement and internal maturation, and if it does not appear to be merely submission to external demands—especially Western demands. There is no more exalted foreign policy task today than to create a dynamic synthesis between the realist and idealist schools of thought.

Epilogue

Dominique Moïsi

Is diplomacy a scientific discipline with well-established and unchanging rules, or is it rather an art that must be practiced delicately, and by professionals? In the wake of the Bir Zeit incident in February 2000 (when Palestinian demonstrators hurled rocks at French prime minister Lionel Jospin to protest against his condemnation of Hezbollah), commentators banded together to criticize a head of government who had stepped into a diplomatic minefield without taking the necessary precautions. In opposition to this traditional attitude, which still dominates in diplomatic circles, is another point of view, according to which, to paraphrase Clemenceau's famous aphorism about war and generals, "diplomacy is too serious to be left to diplomats alone."

I have spent the past twenty years of my professional life at the Institut Français des Relations Internationales (IFRI). IFRI's forerunner, the Centre d'études de politique étrangère, was conceived in the corridors of the Versailles Congress in 1919 and was founded on a Wilsonian view of the world. The First World War, an absurd and suicidal tragedy, resulted largely from the secret diplomacy of states and of the prevailing Alliance system. The victorious Big Powers—France, the United States, Great Britain— owed it to themselves to create independent institutions for research and debate in the field of international relations. Thus were born the Council on Foreign Relations in New York, the Royal Institute of International Affairs (Chatham House) in London, and then, a little later in Paris, the Centre d'études de politique étrangère.

In the age of globalization and the Internet, even though diplomacy has become ever more complex in its many forms and the number of different players has also been growing, the reflections born of the Great War seem more relevant than ever. Has not the globalization of the years 1990–2000 contributed to the emergence of a transnational world, in which states, and thus their representatives—diplomats— remain important actors, but are no longer the only ones on the international stage?

In its almost mathematical simplification of the world, the cold war saw the proliferation of think tanks and "Drs. Strangelove." To practice deterrence with minimal risk, one had to know the rules and ensure that they were shared by one's adversary. Today, strategic issues have increasingly given way to analysis of the interaction of ethnic, social, and economic factors. The cultural dimension of international relations now plays an increasingly important role. An "international civil society" is in the process of being born, albeit in a confused or even dangerously chaotic way.

In this new context, an intellectual, independent, nonpartisan foreign policy—modest but with full freedom of expression—seems more justified than ever. In a homage paid by vice to virtue, it was Talleyrand who, in his 1821 speech on freedom of the press in the Chambre des Pairs, said, "There is someone cleverer than Voltaire, Bonaparte, each of the directors, and each of the past, present and future ministers—it is everyone." Should not this principle apply to international relations?

Often, the testimony and analysis of humanitarian organizations on the ground—or even information gathered and distributed by the media—are at least as important to our understanding of or ways of dealing with particular situations as are the more distant assessments of "professional" diplomats. Nongovernmental research organizations can prove to be as indispensable as the planning and analysis staffs within foreign ministries. Not to mention the personal intuitions of the analysts who, because of their very independence and their "irresponsibility," can allow themselves to "think the unthinkable." This was the case, for example, in September 1989, with Germany's inevitable eventual reunification, while the professional diplomats were all too cautious in their assessments.

In the age of the Internet, cable television with multiple channels, and humanitarian teams on the ground, information is no longer the privilege of an administrative élite to be used only by the state, whose prerogatives—but not responsibilities—are shrinking like leather. Do classified memorandums of the intelligence services contain information that cannot be gleaned from reading and interpreting the work of the quality media? This decentralization of information contains the beginnings of an inevitable revolution: that of managing diplomatic activity. This is a revolution that is already well under way at the Quai d'Orsay, where the pace of activity is accelerating and the centrality of diplomatic decisionmaking is not questioned.

It would be both vain and dangerous to suggest that anyone can make foreign policy. The Internet era does not make everyone an "armchair" diplomat. Not everything is possible. Raison d'état has its own logic that the heart must neither misunderstand nor altogether dominate. Nothing would be more dangerous than to exchange the coldness of an ethic of responsibility for the imperatives of an ethic of conviction monopolized by oppressive and self-designated minorities, with no democratic monitoring, who use their power over the media to impose selective emotions or even particular corporatist, ideological, or other interests.

What is the appropriate relationship between ethics and raison d'état? Can human nature be changed? If man is what he is, diplomacy cannot be anything other than it has always been: not the will to make progress toward the better, on the margins, but the unrewarding and difficult effort to avoid the worst, which is never inevitable but always possible.

In Hubert Védrine's vision of the world as it appears here—though perhaps this is a result of my own questions—is there too much America, seen defensively and emotionally, and not enough Europe, or a Europe that is all too lukewarm?

It is certainly legitimate to emphasize the differences in nature between the monetary arena and the diplomatic one, between the single currency and the Common Foreign and Security Policy. But is this modernized version of the Concert of Nations enough to make Europe credible in the eyes of the world? If two European commissioners today manage to stand out among all the others—the Frenchman Pascal Lamy and the Italian Mario Monti—it is because, beyond their undeniable personal qualities, the former incarnates a Europe that exists and is credible in commercial affairs and the latter exercises real power in the area of competition. Where security and foreign policy questions are concerned, there are too many voices and not enough policy. When the single currency was launched, we talked in France about the euro's "federalizing shock effect," to use Hubert Védrine's expression. But what if it turns out that we are seeing the opposite, whereby the weakness of the euro reflects in part the deficit in the political credibility of the European integration process? There is a striking contrast between the vitality, dynamism, and regained self-confidence of Europe and the majority of its peoples and the near paralysis and identity crisis of the European Union (EU).

We can, of course, regret the hesitant manner in which the United States manages its hyperpower status, alternating between damaging indifference and jealous unilateralism. Surely no other great power in history ever had as much relative power and yet demonstrated so little interest in world affairs. The "emperor" is proud of his superiority, but plans on using it first and foremost to protect himself from the disorder of the empire. And yet, no one can deny that the world would be an infinitely more dangerous and unstable place if it were not for the United States.

We also see, it seems to me, a certain contradiction between the entirely legitimate will to create a multipolar world and the slowness with which Europe is going about overcoming the obvious difficulties with reconciling the deepening and the widening of the European Union. A multipolar world can only begin with Europe's demonstration of its will to play a full role on the international stage, as a complete actor.

Hubert Védrine is obviously right that Europe cannot simply build itself up as the dispenser of lessons in morality to the rest of the world. Europe still exists and thus has interests to defend. But I maintain that today it is realistic to be moral, and not moral to be a realist. To be sure, we live in a world of universal values and selective emotions. And, of course, the moral criteria that apply to great powers, especially nuclear ones, cannot be the same as those that apply to more vulnerable states because they lack size or strategic weight. These double standards must not, however, lead us to facile cynicism. Selective morality is preferable to universal cynicism. It constitutes progress that is, of course, only relative, but it is the first step that counts. Nowhere is sovereignty absolute anymore, just as morality is nowhere entirely pushed aside.

According to Benjamin Disraeli—quoted in André Maurois' biography of that English statesman—"nothing is more disappointing than to be the prime minister of the United Kingdom, but you have to have been the prime minister to know this." Nothing is more frustrating for an analyst of international relations than to serve as a sort of sparring partner for a sitting foreign minister, even one as sophisticated and intellectual as Hubert Védrine. But at the same time, there is nothing more exciting than the feeling of experiencing the development of international affairs, or even an international crisis, from the foreign minister's office—by proxy, or almost like a burglar who happened to be there when the minister had to deal on the spot with the daily reality of international affairs. Thus did we "live together" through the Kosovo war, among other crises, and in retrospect I feel that we shared a common analysis. The way the minister prioritizes—as I perceived it from the things he may have shared with me in confidence or simply from the judgments he made—provides fascinating insight for an "irresponsible" outside analyst like myself. It is sometimes disconcerting, but always exciting.

How can we instill, on the margin, more of a moral code in a world that will always be dominated by the balance of power? This has always been the main inspiration of my passion for international relations. After this dialogue, having had to face the clinical analysis of the practitioner, I can see better than ever the limits and the difficulties of such an approach, but also its necessity. We need a balance between two worlds, so that an observer like myself will not always appear overly idealistic in the eyes of the practitioner, and the practitioner will not seem too steeped in realpolitik in the eyes of the idealists. It's not always easy to be passionately moderate.

HUBERT VÉDRINE

I am convinced that in our era, foreign policy must continually be explained. The public must know how its political leaders look at the world, how they assess the balance of power, and how they see the problems that our foreign policy confronts. The public must know the different options before the country and the reasons for which, at the end of the day, we end up choosing one course of action rather than another.

I put this general principle into practice by speaking regularly before the parliament and its commissions, by agreeing to do interviews as much as my schedule permits, or by making myself available to the press to explain this or that aspect of our policy. But these necessarily brief exercises never, or only rarely, allow me to explain and articulate my thoughts fully. That's why I responded positively to the proposal made to me by Claude Durand, the president of Editions Fayard in Paris, to have this free and open dialogue on all aspects of French foreign policy with a highly respected expert, Dominique Moïsi. We are, of course, playing very different roles here: he's an analyst, and I'm a sitting foreign minister. He has his particular sensitivities and his favorite subjects, and I've got mine, as well as my responsibilities.

We spoke at length and on several different occasions. I don't think we failed to talk about any pressing topic of the day and we spoke freely, often challenging conventional wisdom. I'll be very glad if the short book that has resulted can help contribute to the necessary explanation of our foreign policy.

The first task was to reach agreement about terminology. The public and political debate about France's place and role in the world remains too caught up in nostalgic or emotional reactions. It is handicapped by misplaced sensitivities and obscured by considerations that too often reveal a lack of understanding of the real world or are out of touch with a reality that has changed. All this comes together in the form of a debate about terms. Loaded words, such as "great power," "sovereignty," and "autonomy," among others, are endlessly repeated. This is why we spent so much time trying to come up with just the right words to describe American and French standing in the world, the nature of globalization, and the forces that have been shaping the world. If we all agree on the diagnosis, and if we all use the same words to describe the same things, our country will do better things and will be better understood.

The conclusion of our discussion, of my thinking and my experience after three years as foreign minister, is fundamentally optimistic. France is a great country. It is not going to dissolve into a sort of global magma, or even a European one. France has excellent cards in its hands. If it plays them right, they can be real assets to help preserve, in the best sense of the word, its identity and its influence. France can make a decisive contribution both to a better organization of the world and to the strengthening of Europe. This point is fundamental. We've got to stop swinging back and forth between nostalgia and pretension, which gets us nowhere. France can and must be perfectly at ease in the twenty-first century, conscious of what it represents that is unique, but also open to others, in contact with all the players on the world stage—the 188 other states, the dozens of international institutions, the nongovernmental organizations (NGOs), the big companies, the media. France is a country capable of gaining allies to oppose what is unacceptable and of building consensus around the right ideas. This is an indispensable exercise in an era when it is increasingly rare for a state to decide alone whether to block something or to impose it. France has every reason to be confident and all the necessary means to be bold.

The issue of relations with the United States has for several decades been a problem for our foreign policy. I understand all the reasons that led General de Gaulle, in the context within which he operated, to take the positions that he did. This great tradition has certainly evolved, but it allowed an unfortunate tendency to remain part of our foreign policy toward the United States: a routine and vain aggressiveness that led to nothing and, what's more, compromised our prospects of convincing our other essential partners to undertake anything important with us. It was necessary to go about things differently.

It is true that it is very difficult—to put it mildly—to be the friend and the ally of the American hyperpower without the Americans thinking that we must, for this very reason, automatically align ourselves with them. Our position is clear, however. We believe that in certain cases—indeed, in most cases—we must cooperate with the United States, or support it, simply because we share the same objectives and we work together in the same institutions—the Security Council, the G-8 or the contact group, for example. But on the other hand, we want to be able to express our disagreements with, or even our opposition to, some of its projects or its behavior with the same calm, without these disagreements becoming a major issue or provoking the old refrain of anti-Americanism. So sometimes we cooperate and sometimes we disagree with the United States. I think we have found a balance and that a certain consensus has formed—in any case, in France—around this concept of French-American relations, which is healthier, more frank, more concrete, and more long term.

A number of classical diplomatic questions remain in the world today, whether we're talking about the Balkans, Russia, China, the Near or Middle East, or the African Great Lakes region. I've already talked in some detail about how we're tackling each of them and what we're doing. What I would rather do in this epilogue is to emphasize one fundamental problem and a set of new problems. The fundamental problem is that of the future of the European Union. The new problems are making foreign policy in a globalized world and the renewed relationship between realism and ethics.

The European Union is at a crossroads. This is a cliché, but it precisely describes the current situation, which has two possible outcomes: reinforcement or dilution. The union must expand its membership. There is no legitimate reason to refuse entry to countries that are free from communism, share our values, and are ready and able to make the necessary efforts to adapt to the union's legal, economic, and political rules. But even if well prepared—even well negotiated and thus under control—this big enlargement (going from fifteen to twenty-seven members—one day even thirty or more) radically changes the bases on which European construction was conceived, launched, and successfully developed by the EU's founding fathers and historical leaders, all the way up to and including the ratification of the Maastricht Treaty and the creation of the euro.

It is no longer enough to invoke Robert Schuman's name, to display unshakable European optimism, to make daily calls for boldness, courage, and vision in order to answer this simple question: how can a Europe of thirty be made to work? We already see the problems that a Europe of fifteen confronts. The debate about Europe's organization has now been launched, with two types of proposals—pragmatic and federalist—emerging for the short and the long terms. This is a positive development.

International relations are undergoing a revolution. We have talked about this throughout the discussion. International relations today are no longer simply the sum of bilateral diplomatic relations. There is a difference in nature between the relations maintained among the eight powers of the Congress of Vienna—or even among the fifty-three founding member states of the United Nations at the 1945 San Francisco conference—and the 189 current states, after decolonization, the breakup of the Soviet Union and Yugoslavia, and general decompartmentalization. We have analyzed the beneficial, promising, or negative aspects of this great change and the role of the numerous new actors in international life. Whatever one thinks of these changes, however, French foreign policy must take them into account. These are the new realities that we must integrate into our analyses, the decisions we take, and the implementation of our policies. This is a genuine transformation that has been begun by the entire French Foreign Ministry, which must be a watchtower that follows international developments, a control tower for our international relations, and the orchestrator of the defense of our interests and the promotion of our ideas.

I have explained the ways in which we do this. One of the logical consequences of these innovations is that the entirety of international institutions must be reformed and adapted in the coming years. Beyond what I've already said about the European Union, this is also true for the United Nations (in particular, the Security Council), the international financial institutions (the International Monetary Fund and the World Bank), the World Trade Organization (in particular, concerning the way it does business), etc. All these institutions must become more representative, and thus more legitimate, while remaining or becoming even more effective. In all these areas, France has made proposals and plans to make more of them, either by itself or through the intermediary of the European Union. This is the expression of a political will, which is very strong in France, to "civilize" or "humanize" globalization, or at least to make some rules for it, given that its savage or destructive aspects are as clear as its enriching or liberating dimensions.

Another major question that cuts across the whole spectrum of foreign policy today is that of the relationship between ethics and realism, and we devoted a whole chapter to this. I said in response to Dominique Moïsi's questions and I would like to repeat here, with feeling: I do not believe that there are, on one hand, states—cold monsters inspired by the most cynical realpolitik—and on the other hand, a developing international civil society full of transparency, morality, and justice, that will resolve all the world's problems if only we put our trust in it. I don't feel obliged to defend realism as it is caricatured by idealists. Nor do I want to mock the idealism that makes fatalists roll their eyes. This black-and-white picture does not interest me. What does motivate me is to bring about a synthesis in French foreign policy between historical experience, hardened realism, the strongest and newest moral demands, technological and methodological innovations, principles and actions, memory and vision.

This is a great ambition. Such an objective can never be completely or consistently achieved. But trying to get close to this goal justifies constant effort. All the more so, because this is the expression in foreign policy terms of what the government that I am proud to belong to is accomplishing in all areas. This is why I was more than willing to participate in this discussion, which has been so stimulating and enriching, especially on the most complex issues. And I was very happy that Brookings suggested publishing this book in the United States. I saw this as an opportunity to address myself directly to American readers. (And of course I updated it to take account of the numerous events that took place through spring 2001.) There is not enough dialogue between France and the United States, but when it takes place it is always very interesting and useful. I am happy to contribute to it. I hope it will have become clear how much my views are animated by an ethic of responsibility that, for me, has the power of a conviction.

Index

AFAA. *See* Association française d'action artistique
Afghanistan, 121
Africa: crises, 87–88, 116–17, 119; democratization, 88, 89; development aid, 86, 88, 116; French policies, 116–17; North, 62; relations with EU, 85–90, 116; U.S. policies, 50
Albania, 56
Albright, Madeleine, 10–11, 35, 45, 46, 52, 85, 95
Allègre, Claude, 26
America Online (AOL), 20
Angell, Norman, 7
Arab-Israeli peace process, 90–94, 95–99, 119
Arafat, Yassir, 97
Architecture, 27
Aron, Raymond, 97

ASEAN. *See* Association of Southeast Asian Nations
Asia: human rights abuses, 114–15. *See also specific countries*
Association française d'action artistique (AFAA), 23
Attali, Jacques, 60
Aung San Su Chi, 114–15
Auschwitz, 120
Australia, 5, 26
Austria, 70, 106–07
Authoritarian governments, 105–07, 118

Balkans, 50, 64, 73, 100, 113. *See also* Bosnia-Herzegovina; Kosovo; Yugoslavia
Baltic states, 111
Barak, Ehud, 91, 95
Barnier, Michel, 59

Democracy: in Africa, 88, 89; aspirations to, 101, 102; creation process, 10–11, 103–05, 123; and economic development, 105, 123; in France, 103; and globalization, 9, 10; Kosovo elections, 112; in Latin America, 120; promotion, 39, 106, 113, 116, 120–21; in United States, 4, 51; Warsaw Declaration, 10–12; Western policies, 103–04; in Yugoslavia, 112–13, 114, 119

Democratic Republic of Congo (DRC), 116

Department of International Cooperation and Development (DGCID, France), 21

Diouf, Abdou, 88

Diplomacy, 125–27. *See also* Foreign policy

Disraeli, Benjamin, 129

DRC. *See* Democratic Republic of Congo

Durand, Claude, 130

East Timor, 84, 115

Economic development: aid to Africa, 86, 88, 116; relationship to democratization, 105, 123

Education, 24, 25–26

Edufrance, 26

Egypt, 5, 23–24, 90, 98

Etat de droit, 109–10

Ethics: relationship to raison d'état, 127. *See also* Human rights; Morality

Eurogroup, 74–75

Europe: assets, 29; colonialism, 7; identity, 50; U.S. role, 2. *See also* European Union

European Confederation proposal, 49

European Parliament, 67, 68

European Union (EU): aid to Kosovo, 112; Austrian government and, 70, 106–07; British role, 70; French presidency, 63–67, 72, 109; French priorities, 75; French role, 67, 68–69; German role, 68–69, 70; goals, 55, 73; importance to France, 62–63; institutional reforms, 58, 59–60, 64–67, 68, 69, 133; problems, 128; role in world, 128–29; shape of future, 60–62, 74–75, 132–33; strategic partners, 56, 62. *See also* Foreign policy, European

European Union enlargement: boundaries, 55–56, 62; criteria, 59, 72, 73; cultural issues, 25; debate on, 55–57, 58–59, 64, 71–73; French views, 64, 71–72, 132–33; and institutional reforms, 61, 69; motives of candidates, 49; negotiations, 55, 67, 71, 75, 111; process, 59, 60, 70–71; strategy, 57; Turkey, 55–56, 62, 63–64, 72–73; U.S. views, 56–57

Euro system, 61, 74–75, 78, 79, 128

Films, American, 3, 25, 44, 46, 49

Finland, 111

Fischer, Joschka, 60, 61, 66–67, 69, 70, 85, 99

Foreign Ministry, French: functions, 133; relations with president, 40–41; Service des oeuvres, 23. *See also* Foreign policy, French

Foreign policy: commercial factors, 96; influence of media, 32–34,

Israel, 91; reunification, 127; role in EU, 68–69, 70; role in world, 4; Security Council membership, 5; use of euro, 79; views of EU institutions, 68
Ghana, 88
Girard, René, 3
Giraudoux, Jean, 23
Giscard d'Estaing, Valéry, 90, 91
Globalization: American cultural influence, 3, 4, 19, 20, 25, 44, 46; attitudes in France, 43–44; benefits to U.S., 43–44; critics of, 46; and democratization, 9, 10; economic inequality, 105; effects in France, 17, 45; English language, 20; French concept of, 30; and foreign policy, 126; history, 7–8; injustices, 121; interdependence of states, 8; and legal systems, 26; management of, 14–15, 19, 28, 39, 121, 134; risks and threats, 12–14, 62; technology, 7–8; U.S. role, 3, 17, 43–44, 46; Western dominance, 12. *See also* International civil society; Media
Gonzales, Felipe, 117
Gorbachev, Mikhail, 1, 108, 121
Gore, Albert, Jr., 51
Gracq, Julien, 34
Greece, 84
Green, Rosario, 24
Guéhenno, Jean-Marie, 10

Habibie, B. J., 115
Habré, Hissène, 117
Hague Tribunal, 114, 117, 119
Havel, Vaclav, 49
Holocaust, 120

Houphouët-Boigny, Felix, 88
Hugo, Victor, 23
Human rights, 9; abuses in Burma, 114–15; abuses in Chechnya, 110; contingent aid, 116; history, 37, 101–02; non-Western views, 102; standards externally imposed, 103, 104; UN Commission on, 107, 109; universality, 100–02
Hungary, 121
Huntington, Samuel, 2, 102

ICC. *See* International Criminal Court
Idealism, 123, 130, 134
IFRI. *See* Institut Français des Relations Internationales
IMF. *See* International Monetary Fund
India, 4, 5, 13
Indonesia, 5, 82, 115
Information: decentralization, 8, 127. *See also* Media
Institut Français des Relations Internationales (IFRI), 125
International civil society, 7, 8–10, 32, 33, 126, 134. *See also* Nongovernmental organizations
International Criminal Court (ICC), 12, 114, 116, 118, 119
International Monetary Fund (IMF), 15, 115, 121, 133
International Organization of the Francophonie, 22–23
International relations: categories of states, 2–6; decompartmentalization, 2, 8, 133; diplomacy, 125–27; post–cold war, 1–2, 18–19; transnational actors, 6–7; U.S.